THE BOOK OF
WATCHET & WILLITON REVISITED

A Past and Present Pictorial Portrait

MAURICE & JOYCE CHIDGEY AND BEN NORMAN

HALSGROVE

Title page: *Swillbridge House, Doniford, in the 1920s.*
It was at one time the residence of Major-General L.C. Dunsterville,
eminent soldier and the model for Kipling's famous character 'Stalky'.

British Library Cataloguing-in-Publication Data.
A CIP record for this title is available from the British Library.

ISBN 978 1 84114 628 7

HALSGROVE

Halsgrove House
Ryelands Industrial Estate
Bagley Road
Wellington
Somerset TA21 9PZ
Tel: 01823 653777
Fax: 01823 216796
email: sales@halsgrove.com
website: www.halsgrove.com

Printed and bound in Great Britain by
CPI Antony Rowe Ltd, Chippenham, Wiltshire

Whilst every care has been taken to ensure the accuracy of the
information contained in this book, the publisher disclaims responsibility
for any mistakes which may have been inadvertently included.

Contents

Acknowledgements

We are very appreciative of all the help, kindness and hospitality shown during the compilation of this book, without which publication would not have been possible. Every effort has been made to be accurate using the information received, but apologise in the event of any errors or omissions. We would like to express our sincere thanks to the present and former people of this very special area of West Somerset, and hope you enjoy your book!

Gratefully acknowledged are the following for the loan of photographs, other material and information: Duncan Stafford, Keith Towells, Pamela Stephens, Elizabeth Cain, David Milton, the late Emily Stark, Roy Dennett, Ann Bryant, John Cridge, Peter Swann, Mary Slade, Phil Watts (Nailsea), John Tennant, the late George May, the late Peter Williamson, Roger and Eileen Risdon, Bonnie Bindon, Shirley Williams, David Sully MBE, Marjorie Hann, Alec and Bernice Danby, Edwin May, David Bulpin, Gordon and Pat Bryant, Norman Ackland, Violet Woods, Marjorie Coles, Fred Bacon, David Langdon, Peter and Betty Armstrong, Michael and Wendy Chapman, Nigel and Margaret Edwards, Ivy Stephenson, the late Bill Pugsley, Nick and Julie Sully, Frances Napper, Evelyn Watts, Norah Linck, Percy Long, Deric and Doreen Gibbons, Laurence Chorley, Joyce Newsham, Norman Morse, Margaret Voss, Steve and Janet Groves, Richard Bulpin, George Haller, Alan Burge, Elizabeth Cooper, Clifford and Joyce Milton, Ray Braunton, Joan Boots, Michael Binding, Adrian Rowe, Douglas Edwards, Steve Guscott, Michael Jones, June Sullivan, Joyce Gibbins, John Coombs, Roger Wedlake, Tony Knight, Linda Norman, Sophie Prole, Phyllis Pugsley, Lilian Downer, Vernon Stone, Moger Woolley DL, Alison Champion, June Roberts, Roger Willis, Glynis Maule, Ann Bishop, Frank Webber, Valerie Norman MBE, Clayton Williams, Simon Bale, Mervyn Parsons, Diana Bale, Hugh Amery, Roy Heard, Elma Hawkins, Patrick Cook, Nigel Swinburn, Frank Collingson, Madge Abbey, Iris Haller, Mark Mossman, Malcolm Bale, Martin Newman, Roy Date, Margaret Clayton, Mavis Towells, Margaret Rigden, Shaun Anning, Michael and Helen McDermaid, Jean Howe MBE, AirPic, Jessie Norman, R. Werren, R.J. Sellick, Raymond Clavey, the late Robin Madge, Janet Strong, David Banks, John Bruford, the late Tom Head, Jenny Taylor, Paul Challice, Sue Upstone, Sheila Clavey, Edward Martin, Philip Perry, Bill Date, Paul Norton, Eileen Woods MBE, Ron Copp, Barry Norman, Sue Williams, Tony Sully, Dudley Binding, Joy Putt, Peter Hesp, West Somerset Rural Life Museum, Allerford, Clifford Beaver, the late George Wyndham, the late Mrs B. Mason, Dean & Dyball, Watchet Town Council, the late Adrian Chidgey, the late Vera Kirby, Steve Yeandle, Derek Quint, Mary Parkman, Richard Ley and the late James Date.

Special thanks for assistance are due to Chris Boyles, Jack Binding, Roy Chave, Michael Sully and Edna Dixon. Thanks also to the editor of the *West Somerset Free Press*, the Somerset Records Office and the Somerset Studies Library.

Two maps are reproduced from the *Victoria County History of the County of Somerset*, vol. V (London 1985), pages 142 and 147, by permission of the Executive Editor; two photographs by permission of Somerset Archaeological and Natural History Society, and photographs of John Short with Revd Dr Allen Brockington and of Cecil Sharp by courtesy of the English Folk Dance and Song Society.

Lastly, we extend thanks to Steven Pugsley, Katy Charge and the staff at Halsgrove for all their help and advice.

Maurice and Joyce Chidgey and Ben Norman, 2007

Introduction

This book is an attempt to portray life, mostly pictorially, down through the years based on the large old geographic parish of St Decuman's – now, of course, two separate parishes, both ecclesiastically and civicly. The detailed histories of both Watchet and Williton have been fully and extensively covered in previous books and a repetition has not been attempted here. What follows is largely a fresh pictorial study covering a wide aspect of local places, people, events and sport down through the years, complemented by a folk story or two. Many of the pictures appear grouped under various themes, while others are simply presented in what might be considered a sort of local photo album in no particular order.

The changes over the past hundred years or so have been staggering, especially the transformation of Watchet's working harbour into a marina, the long-gone grim days of the Williton Workhouse and the digging of roads by manual labour. Even in the lifetime of the authors, villagers could be seen with jugs in hands collecting fresh milk from Jones's dairy in Williton and Watchet townsfolk enjoying the locally-made ice-cream and milk shakes at Mill Farm Dairy Milk Bar. Another long-gone feature of Williton life was when fishermen of Watchet and Minehead called from door to door selling their freshly-caught Watchet sprats and Minehead herrings. These were regarded as a great delicacy and quickly sold. Deliveries by horse and cart are also in the past, likewise the fetching and carrying of gravel from Doniford beach for building purposes. Disappeared also are the Williton Whit Monday gymkhanas and Whitelegge's fun fair on Watchet Esplanade during August, both of which attracted hundreds of people. However, Watchet's longstanding annual summer carnival is still a great attraction and has progressed into a weekend festival. As this book goes to print, Watchet sees major new developments with the enhancement and regeneration of the Esplanade and the development of the East Quay. It is to be hoped these new phases in the town's history will help it reach its full potential for the benefit of residents and visitors alike.

Significant changes have been made in local government and parish boundaries, agriculture, industry and transport; also ecclesiastically, socially and educationally. There has always been great sporting rivalry between Watchet and Williton, with the latter being good-humouredly known as 'the enemy over the hill'. It is heartening that Williton Cricket Club has been reformed and that cricket matches will again be played on the Recreation Ground. Watchet is also well known for its profuse use of nicknames for its townsfolk. The population of the area covered by the old St Decuman's parish has more than doubled since 1902, resulting in a large amount of building development.

St Decuman's Church, c.1900. Note the lamps on top of the entrance pillars.

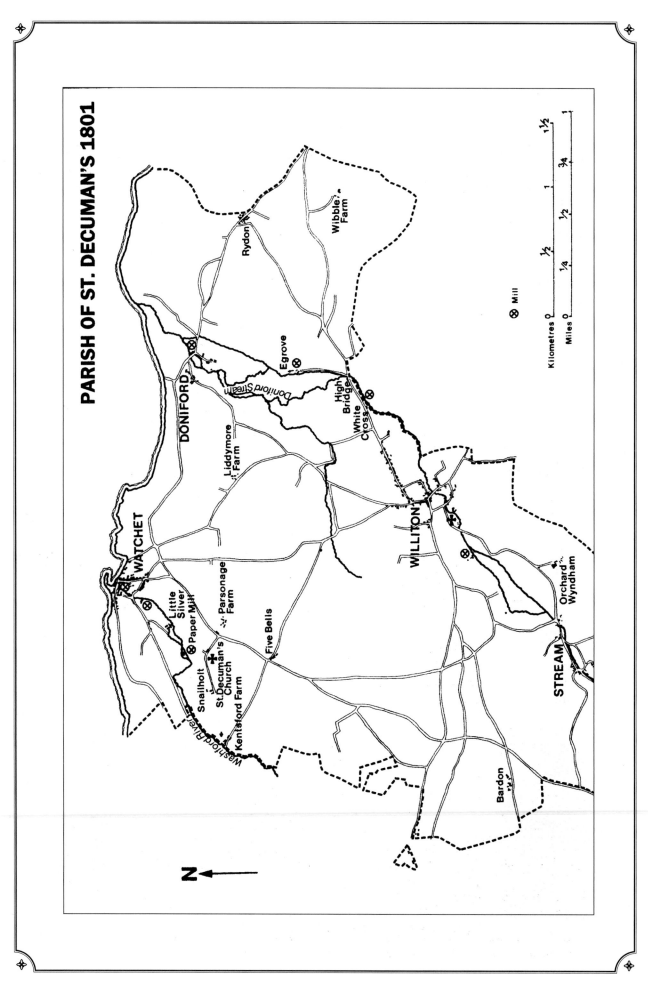

PARISH OF ST. DECUMAN'S 1801

Chapter 1
Outline and Development

Named after the patron saint of its church, the old parish of St Decuman's occupied the coastal plain at the mouth of a broad valley between the Quantocks and the Brendons. On the coast in the north-west corner of the parish is the former borough and market town of Watchet, and two miles south on the southern boundary lies the large village of Williton. Hamlets and farms were scattered throughout the parish and by the seventeenth century Doniford, Bardon and Stream were the principal hamlets. In 1882 a detached part of Nettlecombe was absorbed into St Decuman's and in the same year part of Washford with seven houses, formerly part of St Decuman's, was transferred to Old Cleeve. Parts of St Decuman's parish in the Brendons were transferred to Nettlecombe in 1883 and to Old Cleeve in 1886. In 1894 the rural district of Williton was formed and St Decuman's Parish Council created. The parish was divided in 1902 and Watchet urban district (probably the smallest urban district authority in the country) was formed, with the remainder of the ancient parish becoming the separate civil parish of Williton.

In 1974 the two areas became constituent parishes in the West Somerset district, with Watchet having a Town Council and Williton retaining its Parish Council. Williton then became the centre for much of the administration of West Somerset District Council. Boundary changes were also made in the early 1980s, including the transfer of Rydon to West Quantoxhead. The total population of St Decuman's parish in 1801 was 1,602 rising to 3,302 by 1901. Watchet's population was 1,936 in 1931 and had increased to 4,400 by 2002; Williton's totalled 1,161 in 1931 and 2,710 in 2002. Besides the expansion of Watchet and Williton in the last and present centuries, two other areas of growth have been Five Bells and Doniford, where the Swill or Swilly river runs into the sea. In 1925 there was another milestone in local history with the arrival of the military at Doniford, a link which was to last for 45 years.

North of Williton is a site named Battlegore where a battle against invading Danes is said to have taken place in AD918. An archaeological dig took place there in 1931, but nothing of any significance was found. When Watchet folk good-humouredly boast about their sporting prowess over Williton, the inevitable retort they get is: 'But it was the Williton lads who sent the Danes packing at Battlegore!'

Prophetess Mother Shipton's tomb in Blackdown Wood, between Williton and Yarde, has been shown to be a copy of one in the North of England. Nevertheless, one of her legendary prophecies has been passed down by generations of Williton and Watchet folk:

> Watchet and Doniford both shall drown,
> And Williton become the seaport town.

Yet despite considerable coastal erosion over the years, Watchet and Doniford still remain very much in evidence!

St Decuman's Church, so dedicated probably in 1189, is one of the largest and finest in West Somerset. Situated in a commanding position overlooking Watchet, it is this prominence which helped inspire Coleridge whilst staying with Wordsworth at the Bell Inn in 1797 with the first verses of *The Rime of the Ancient Mariner*, considered among the greatest works in English literature. It was also the mother church of Williton (now its own parish). The date in which St Decuman lived is uncertain; some say AD400, others about AD700. He was said to be a Welsh missionary who crossed the Bristol Channel on a wattle or hurdle and lived a hermit's life in the neighbourhood of Watchet. Legend has it that whilst praying one day, a native came behind him and cut

The interior of St Decuman's Church. Note the ornate brass gas lamps.

St Decuman's Holy Well.

off his head, after which he raised himself up, took his head in his hands, and carried it to the spring just below the church. There he washed all traces of blood from his body and head before replacing it and then continued with his missionary work. The spot is now the Holy Well.

Another tradition relating to the church is that the inhabitants desired to build it nearer to Williton than its present site. This was objected to by a certain gentleman who disliked churches, and night after night he carried stones which workmen had laid during the day from the selected site to the present one. The conflict went on so long that the inhabitants gave up the thought of building on the site they desired and the church was erected on its present site.

Probably Celtic in origin, the present Church of St Decuman has no features datable from before the late-thirteenth century. The first named prebendary is N. de Evesham in 1248. The gift by Simon Brito (or Brett) in 1190 to Wells Cathedral of the Church of St Decuman for a perpetual prebend of the church of Wells is probably the earliest documentary evidence regarding the church. Next comes the gift by Robert Fitzurse to the Church of St Decuman of 20 acres of land and 2.5 acres of meadow. These happenings, which took place between 1190 and 1205 were after the murder of the Archbishop of Canterbury, Thomas á Becket, in his own cathedral in 1170, when two of the four knights who murdered Becket were Sir Richard de Brett of Sampford Brett and Sir Reginald Fitzurse of Williton. Before 1172 Sir Reginald Fitzurse divided the manor of Williton into two – giving one half to his brother Robert and the other half to the Knights Templar, perhaps as a penance for his part in the murder. After the murder the four knights were sent on a penitential crusade to the Holy Land by the Pope, but all died within five years and were buried in Jerusalem.

The church was repaired and restored in 1886 at a considerable cost and many other improvements were made in 1896. The Wyndham pew stands in the north chapel with tombs and monuments of that family. The tower, which has six bells, bears a figure which may be a representation of St Decuman.

The Holy Cross Chapel is situated on the upper floor of the Market House in Market Street. The original chapel was probably in existence in the early-fourteenth century, but by 1830 it was in ruins.

St Peter's, Williton, is now the church of an ecclesiastical parish, formerly being a chapelry dependent on St Decuman's. Robert Fitzurse is said to have re-built the chapel at Williton in about 1200 and the Prebendary of St Decuman's was instructed to find a chaplain to serve it. The churchwardens of St Decuman's administered the parish in two parts – the Williton side and the Watchet side – by the latter part of the sixteenth century, and after 1784 chaplains were called perpetual curates or vicars, appointed by successive vicars of St Decuman's. Separate registers

St Peter's Church, Williton, before its enlargement in 1857. FROM THE PIGOTT DRAWING BY J. BUCKLER, 1837.

began in 1792. By the early-fourteenth century, St Peter's Chapel was dedicated to All Saints. The Revd Samuel J. Heathcote (vicar from 1854–1906) was responsible for much restoration work on the church from 1856–59. Burials always took place at St Decuman's churchyard until its closure and then at the Watchet cemetery, which opened in 1993, although a few took place at Williton in the eighteenth century. However, in 2004 a small garden of rest was dedicated next to St Peter's Church where ashes can be scattered or buried.

In about 1766 Protestant Nonconformity was introduced to Watchet by Lady Huntingdon's preachers and preaching was continued there and at Williton by student ministers. A Baptist chapel was built in Watchet in 1824 and stood prominently above the town; it was used for many years. In 1813 the Watchet Baptist minister was holding meetings in Robert Street, Williton, and later a site was acquired in Catwell and a chapel opened in 1844. Services were discontinued at Williton in 1919 and a disused railway carriage used as a mission room at Doniford was closed in about 1920.

In 1803 John Date's house at Watchet was licensed for worship, the licence application being supported by John and Mary Stoate, John Wood and Date himself. They were members of families prominent both in local Methodism and in the business life of Watchet. In 1824 a chapel was built off Swain Street and remained in use until the present building was

Disused railway carriage used as a Baptist Mission Room at Doniford; services were discontinued in the 1920s.

Painting of Watchet Harbour, c.1708. COURTESY OF THE WYNDHAM FAMILY.

erected in Station Road (now Harbour Road) in 1871. There were Methodist meetings at the paper mills in the 1860s and in 1883 the former Anglican chapel at Brendon Hill was brought to the mills. A Methodist chapel was built in Williton in 1820 in an alley off Fore Street, being replaced in 1883 by the present building at the foot of Tower Hill.

A chapel called the Temple was opened in Watchet in 1860 by the Bible Christians and later became part of the United Methodist movement. Services ceased there in 1962, the building becoming incorporated into St Decuman's C. of E. School and later became the Watchet Boxing Club's training quarters.

The Salvation Army came to Watchet in 1882 and was formally established in 1884. They now occupy a citadel near the railway station, having until 1928 occupied the former Methodist chapel in Swain Street, then known as Castle Hall.

The first mention of Watchet's harbour is recorded in about 1250 and in 1458 its little breakwater and most of the houses around it were washed away in a storm. Further storms caused great damage in 1659 and 1661. In 1708 Sir William Wyndham built a new harbour costing £1,000, which was similar in design to the one now at Minehead. The Esplanade was built in 1843 by the fourth Earl of Egremont, who at that time was lord of the manor.

By the year 1855 the export of thousands of tons of iron ore from the Brendon Hills necessitated enlargement of the harbour and this was financed by private investors. The new harbour, which included an east pier and wharf, was constructed in 1861–62 by James Abernethy. Harbour trade then flourished and Watchet prospered. In December 1900 came disaster – the harbour was hit by a raging sea swept on by terrific westerly gale-force winds. Ships were smashed like matchwood and sails ripped to ribbons. The horrendous damage to the harbour and ships is vividly described in the book *Tales of Watchet Harbour*.

With the formation of Watchet Urban District in

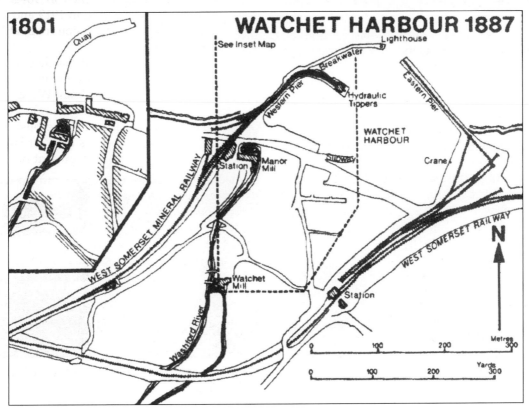

The gale-damaged west breakwater and extension at Watchet harbour, 1900.

1902, and through indomitable community spirit, the harbour was rebuilt and the town's industries and people's livelihoods were saved. After many years of shipping business, harbour trade declined in the 1990s and 1993 saw the closure of the harbour to shipping; in 2001 Watchet began a new maritime venture with the opening of a marina.

In the eighteenth century new street names suggest in-filling between the river and Swine (later Swain) Street – Silver Street by 1746, Back Lane (later Back Street and later still Anchor Street), and Keck Alley Street in 1824. The town began to expand westwards in West Street by the 1850s, but principally over the fields to the south and east overlooking the harbour. In 1859 Causeway Terrace was built and Temple Villas and Temple Terrace were so called after the Bible Christian chapel, built in 1860. Almyr and Wristland Terraces were named after the former open fields on which they stood.

Manors and estates in the parish were Williton (sometimes referred to as the manor of Williton and Watchet), Williton Fulford, Williton Hadley, Williton Temple, Williton Hospital, Williton Regis, Doniford, Hartrow and Doniford (Court Farm probably being the Doniford manor-house), Orchard, Watchet, Kentsford, Culvercliffe Watchet, Watchet with the Members, Watchet Haweye, Little Silver and Bardon.

Orchard Wyndham, c.1930.

Most of the above either descended or were absorbed into the Wyndham estates, with the Wyndhams, whose family home is at Orchard Wyndham, near Williton, becoming the major landowners in the parish. Kentsford was the manor-house of Watchet and is its oldest residence.

Thomas Blinman, newly-appointed curate of Williton in 1575, was licensed to teach boys there, and Robert Parsons the younger, minister of the parish 1643–62, began teaching at the grammar school in St Decuman's in 1636. A school was kept in the priest's house at Williton in 1802 and another school was opened in Williton in 1811. Supported by subscriptions and intended for children of labouring men 'with no apparent prospect of education', it was known as the Free School of Williton. It closed in 1821 because of the reluctance of the poor to attend. A Methodist established a day- and boarding-school at Watchet in 1826, and by 1835 there were eight day-schools and four Sunday schools in the parish. In 1851 there were at least five schools – a Wesleyan Sunday school and a boys' boarding-school at Sea View Terrace, both in Watchet, and a day-school, Baptist Sunday school and a school in the Workhouse at Williton. New National School buildings were opened in Williton in 1872 and an undenominational school opened in Watchet in 1869–70. A new Church of England School was built at Watchet in 1873.

The two schools in Watchet and the National School at Williton were absorbed into the County Council system in 1903. At Watchet the undenominational school became a Council School, then having an average attendance of 125 boys and girls and 39 infants. The Watchet National School (known locally as the Church School) assumed aided status and had 135 boys and girls and 100 infants on its books. With 116 boys and girls and 80 infants the Williton school was slightly smaller. All three schools were retained when a secondary modern school was built at Williton in 1957 for pupils over 11 years. From 1959 the Watchet National School was known as St Decuman's C. of E. School. In 1971 further reorganisation converted Williton Secondary School into a middle school for pupils aged 9–14, and was subsequently known as Danesfield Church of England School. The three contributing schools at Watchet and Williton were converted into first schools. Later the two Watchet schools were closed and replaced with a new school, named Knights Templar CE and Methodist Community VA First School, which was officially opened in 1990 under the headship of Mr Alan Woollam. The Church School was used as a Baptist church for a while, but eventually it was demolished like the Council School and both sites became housing projects. A new St Peter's First School was opened at Williton in 1996.

Knights Templar School Hall fund-raising committee with a £25,000 cheque as a result of their appeal in 1989. The final total raised was over £32,000, which provided a larger hall, balcony, equipped the users' kitchen, curtains and refurbished chairs. Left to right: *Sadie Cowan, Jackie White, Fran Kirk, Pat Tew (secretary), Marilyn Binding (treasurer), Nigel Edwards, Tony Knight (chairman), John Parfitt (Diocesan Board of Finance), Alan Woollam (headmaster).*

From the later nineteenth century there were several private schools in the parish, including a girls' school at Temple Way, Watchet. The Misses Green had established a school for girls at The Poplars at Higher Stream, near Williton, by 1889 and this was still in being in 1910. There were two private schools at Watchet in the 1920s and 1930s known as Westcliffe and St Decuman's. From about 1927 there was a school for girls in Williton, which was later known as Beaconwood Private School. After it closed in about 1940 it became the Beaconwood Dairy. Situated on Tower Hill, Williton, there was a boys' preparatory school called St Decuman's, which was open from the 1930s until the 1950s. Founded in 1955, Buckland School at Watchet is a private day school for boys and girls.

Of prime importance in the parish was agriculture and by 1841 farming units had achieved a stable pattern, the largest being Doniford Farm (250 acres), followed by Rydon (163 acres), Snailholt (143 acres) and Kentsford (131 acres). Bridge, Mill, Higher and Lower Stream, Egrove and Wibble Farms amounted to over 70 acres each, but within the next decade Bridge Farm had extended to 250 acres and Egrove to 156 acres. In 1851, 119 men and 17 boys were regularly employed on the farms of the parish.

Paper-making has been the main life-blood of the Watchet economy, giving employment to thousands of people over the years. In the mid-nineteenth century mariner or sailor was the commonest occupation in Watchet and there were several shipowners, three mariner store dealers, a ship builder and a ship broker, as well as coastguards and a lifeboat station. There were 21 master mariners, ten shipowners and three shipbrokers by 1875.

Harbour trade at Watchet in the twentieth century consisted mainly of coal, woodpulp, esparto grass, paper, grain and feed stuffs, flour, timber, motor parts, tractors, container, and small quantities of scrap iron, among other things.

Fishing has always been an important and popular part of the Watchet economy, and seaweed has been collected commercially along the shore at Doniford.

In 1855 the West Somerset Mineral Railway was founded to carry iron ore from the Brendon Hill mines to Watchet for shipment to South Wales. It was not used officially for passenger traffic until some years later. The mines were closed in 1882, but were reopened in 1907, but a slump in the steel industry led to the mines being finally closed in 1909. The rails were taken up during the First World War.

The broad gauge West Somerset Railway was opened from Taunton in 1862 with a terminus at Watchet; its extention to Minehead in 1874 greatly increased the influx of tourists to the area. Between the two world wars many local people took advantage of a special Saturday evening excursion to Taunton called the 'bacon train' to secure late-night shopping bargains. The line closed in 1971, but was partially reopened by a private company in 1975. Watchet and Williton stations were reopened a year later and the line was further extended to Bishops Lydeard in 1979. At the time of writing it looks very likely that the line will reach its ultimate destination of Taunton and offer a regular service from there to Minehead. It is the longest private line in the country offering steam and diesel services.

Williton remained the centre of a farming community, but after the creation of a new road from Bridgwater and the opening of the Union Workhouse there in 1838 its commerical life increased. The *West Somerset Free Press*, a weekly newspaper, was founded there in 1860 and continues to be published. With its expansion and retention as an administrative centre, Williton has become quite an important local shopping centre, serving the outlying district as well as the village, but the tremendous increase in traffic

Above: West Somerset Free Press *offices and The Royal Huntsman, Williton, 2002.*

Below: *Watchet's old Market House (now the Museum on the ground floor with Holy Cross Chapel above), which housed A.E. Organ's ironmongery in the 1920s.*

has caused some problems. Among older properties in the village, Long Street still retains Honeysuckle Cottage (a small medieval hall-house) and Arden Cottage (dating from the fourteenth century).

By 1222 a market had been established at Watchet and in 1311 Shambles in the centre of the market place were mentioned. They were replaced in 1819–20 by the Market House, a two-storeyed stone building with open arches to the ground floor and an open staircase at its west end to the upper floor, under which was the Court Leet lockup. The ground floor was later converted to a shop, but at the time of writing is the home of the Market House Museum, which was opened in 1979 by Mr George Wyndham. Its inception was due mainly to the forethought and effort of the late Leslie Wedlake (first curator), Ben Norman, Michael Sully, Malcolm Brown, Eileen Woods, Richard Werren, Harold Turner, Ethel Kirby, Roger Wedlake, etc, along with the generous help of Mr Wyndham. Much of the museum's success is due to a large band of voluntary stewards who supervise an annual total in excess of 40,000 visitors during its seven months of opening. The upper floor was used as a mission church and is now the Holy Cross Chapel. The market was held on Saturdays and continued until the 1830s.

St Decuman's had a fair by 1244, held on a site between the church and the prebendal house (later Parsonage Farm) in a field known as Twyfayrecroftes in the fourteenth century and as Fair Close in the nineteenth century. The fair for cattle and all sorts of

goods was held on 24 August, but was discontinued in 1819. A fair for hardware and toys was held at Williton on Trinity Monday in 1767, but was discontinued in 1877. Cattle fairs or sales and new markets were established at Williton in the nineteenth century, but had ceased by 1948.

By 1321 there were four mills in the parish – one was the manorial mill at Williton (later Egrove Mill), one probably the town mill at Watchet, one at Stream and the fourth was held by Edmund Martin, a tenant of Williton manor. Egrove was a fulling (cloth) mill in 1712, but by 1721 was occupied by John Rayner, of Bristol, as a paper mill. The lease later passed to a Bristol surgeon and paper-making continued with William Wood, of Snailholt paper mills, in charge of production in 1816. Paper-making ceased there in 1847 and towards the end of the nineteenth century it became a grist (grain) mill. Milling ceased at the town mill at Watchet, near the mouth of the Washford river, in 1911 and the site is now occupied by a private house. By 1318 a fulling mill was established in Watchet, later known as Little Silver. The mill passed to Richard Gimblett in 1807, but fulling was discontinued soon after that date, although the mill may have been used for a time from 1824 to dress cloth made by the poor. The mill was replaced in 1832 by a new building further downstream occupied by Thomas Stoate, a flour miller. Also occupying the town mills, the Stoates closed both in 1911 after a fire at their new mill and transferred the business to Bristol. In 1916 the building was reconstructed and occupied by the Exmoor Paper and Bag Company, which ceased production around 1960, and at the time of writing the premises are in multiple occupation.

A fulling and grist mill was held by the Wyndham estate in 1587, but by 1652 it was producing paper for John Saffyn, of Cullompton, Devon. It was described as Snailholt, near the site of the present Wansbrough Paper Mill. By 1727 the tenant was John Wood, the first of four generations of that family to work the mill. Sir John Wyndham was said to have built two grist mills near his manor of Williton in 1617 (perhaps the origin of Orchard Mills?). Milling continued at Orchard Mill until 1967, and at present the site houses a Bakelite museum. A fulling mill had been built at Doniford by 1545, but a grist mill was still in use in 1623; cloth was made there in the eighteenth and nineteenth centuries. The buildings, standing by a leat fed by the Swill river and adjoining fields called Rack Meadow, included a miller's house, which now comprise two houses called Swillbridge House and Ivy Cottage.

Watchet was described as a borough in 1243, being owned by Sir Ralph Fitzurse, and in 1302 the borough was represented in Parliament. The records of Watchet Borough Court or Court Leet date from 1273 and survive spasmodically until 1606 and from 1620 until the present. Meetings are held annually in

The water-wheel which powered the old mill at Bridge Farm, Williton, c.1940s.

Market Street, Watchet, in the 1920s, showing the Bell Inn on the left and the London Inn further down on the opposite side.

October at the Bell Inn. A similar Court Leet was held at Williton in the title of the Manors of Williton Regis, Williton Hadley and Williton Fulford, but meetings ceased in 1953.

In 1857 a police station and court house were built at Williton, though there have been no court hearings there for several years. A parish fire service was established in 1855–56, public lighting in 1867, and a water undertaking in 1889. In later years there were fire brigades at both Watchet and Williton, but at the time of writing only the latter survives.

The oldest named inn in Watchet was the Three Mariners, which stood on the south side of the market place by 1657 and continued into the eighteenth century. Mentioned in 1707 was the Blue Anchor, which survived until after 1807. Three other inns in the earlier eighteenth century were the Black Boy (washed away by 1738), the White Hart and the Bell (probably a new name for the former Three Mariners). There were seven licensed houses in the parish as a whole in 1736 and 11 in 1755. By 1787 there were eight inns in Watchet: the Greyhound, George, Ship, Jolly Sailor, Royal Oak and the New Inn to add to the two earlier inns (the Bell and the Blue Anchor). The New Inn, White Hart, Ship and Jolly Sailor all stood on the quay, facing the north side of the market place. The Bell, Greyhound, Anchor (recorded in 1800) and the George were the only survivors by 1818. The London (for a short period known as The Clipper) is first found in 1822, the Star in 1825 and the Sailor's Delight in 1840. The George had closed by 1841, but the Greyhound survived until after 1861, when business was transferred to the New Commercial, later the West Somerset Commercial (or Mossman's) Hotel. The Wellington (1861) and the Railway (1866) only survived for short periods. The Castle Temperance Hotel was established by 1889 and the Anchor was offering accommodation for tourists by 1894. The Bell, the London, the Anchor, the Star and the West Somerset Hotel are the town's surviving historic inns at the time of writing.

The Blue Anchor, an ale house at Williton, was built in the fifteenth century; this was increased in size and re-named the Coach and Horses in the early-eigh-

teenth century. It was enlarged again in 1830 and became the Wyndham Hotel, but its name was changed again in 1842 to the Egremont Hotel. The hotel closed in 2003 and was converted into homes. Other inns were the Pelican (1686), Red Lion (1736), New Inn and King's Arms (both 1787). The Red Lion and King's Arms had gone by 1800 and the Wyndham Arms had been opened. The Lamb (1850) was renamed Railway Hotel (now the Foresters Hotel) in 1858 and the New Inn is now known as the Royal Huntsman. The Mason's Arms, formerly a beer shop, occupied the former Shutgate toll-house by 1866. It is pleasing to note that the name Shutgate has been revived by the naming of a nearby housing estate Shutgate Meadow.

Friendly Societies in the parish included a club at Williton by 1815 and the Social Order Benefit Society in 1820. At Watchet the Re-Union Club was establised in 1849 and branches of national friendly societies such as the Foresters and various temperance societies were also in existence. Founded at Watchet in 1863, the United Sailors' Society regularised a long-established pilotage system known later as the Watchet Hobblers Association. An annual regatta and a local custom called 'Caturn's Night' (25 November) were part of Watchet's social life in the late-nineteenth century. Caturn's Night was also celebrated in Williton with goodly helpings of hot cakes and cider.

One of Watchet's finest assets was instigated in 1922 when Mr William Wyndham leased land to trustees for the War Memorial Ground. A fine pavilion was opened in 1929, followed by further developments over the years. Watchet Urban District Council became the trustees in 1962; it then passed on to West Somerset District Council, who subsequently handed the juristiction of the ground to Watchet Town Council. Williton is also fortunate to possess a fine War Memorial Recreation Ground for sporting and other outdoor events, thanks again to the generosity of Mr William Wyndham and the voluntary hard work of local ex-Servicemen in the early 1920s to make it a fitting memorial to fallen comrades; it is now administered by the Parish Council and has trustees who are also parish councillors.

SAINT DECUMAN'S CHARITY.

Rules to guide the Annual Distribution of . . Blankets. . .

The following Persons are to receive Blankets, subject to the discretion of the Churchwardens:

1.—Married Couples, as and when the number of their Children increases — *One every Second Year.*

2.—Married Couples, Widowers, and Widows, with Young Children under the age of twelve years, dependent on them respectively—*One every Third Year.*

3.—Married Couples, Widowers, and Widows, without Children dependent on them, and Single Men and Women wholly or partially disabled respectively—*One every Fourth Year.*

Dated this 1st day of December, 1908.

The foregoing Rules shall be subject to the following Exceptions and Qualifications, viz.:

No Person shall be entitled to a Blanket—

1.—Who shall have resided permanently beyond the limits of the Ecclesiastical Parish of St. Decuman's within the period of three years immediately preceding the date of his or her application.

2.—Or who shall be a Master Tradesman or other Person employing hands or shall be a person whose income or wages shall in the opinion of the Churchwardens render Charity unnecessary.

3.—Or who shall be found to have sold or otherwise disposed of a Blanket which he or she shall have received from this Charity in some previous year.

4.—Or who shall neglect to make personal application for a Blanket.

NOTE.—In exceptional circumstances the Churchwardens reserve the right to depart from any of these Rules.

BY ORDER OF THE CHURCHWARDENS,

JOYCE, RISDON, & HOSEGOOD,
Secretaries & Treasurers.

In 1583 the churchwardens and sidesmen of St Decuman's held approximately 15 acres of land and other property. Income from this was applied to the repair of the Parish Church, the maintenance of soldiers, supporting the poor, or payment of charges on the parish. By 1901 the St Decuman's Charity, as it was called, comprised the stock, just over six acres of land, ten houses and cottages, and a printing office, as well as the stock of other charities. From real property there was a net income of £103 and from investments, £33.9s.4d. Blankets were distributed to 168 people, the date for distribution of these being commonly known as 'blanket day'. Coal vouchers replaced blankets in 1939, and grocery vouchers were given in the 1970s, each being worth £3 in 1979. All but one cottage had been sold by 1977, and investments produced an income of approximately £1,100. This was applied to the repair of the Parish Church and in distributions to the old, the widowed and the infirm of Watchet and Williton. In 1999 a change was made in the constitution of the charity when it was registered as St Decuman's Parish Trust with ten trustees appointed to supervise funds for the general benefit of poor persons. Mary Huxtable Sutton, of Minehead, bequeathed four houses and £1,100 to the trustees of St Decuman's Charity in 1935 to establish and endow almshouses, the money to build small houses for needy labouring men or women, the existing houses for those not of the labouring class. In 1937 a pension charity was established from the sale proceeds of two of the houses, but no other houses were built. In 1975 the accumulated funds of the two charities were combined to form the Mary Huxtable Sutton Relief-in-Need charity, payable to any living person within six miles of Watchet and not under 55 years. The trustees agreed in 1979 to a maximum annual distribution of £200 to all recipients. This is a separate charity, but is administered by the same trustees as St Decuman's Parish Trust.

Chapter 2

WATCHET

Maritime

A Seafaring Heritage

A fair-size brig awaits the tide in Watchet harbour. Five smaller vessels wait to be loaded at the iron ore jetty, c.1862.

This interesting photograph of the harbour, c.1887, shows a ketch and a schooner alongside the iron-ore jetty (top centre). The shipment of ore from Watchet by this time had ceased, but the jetty was still in use for the import of timber and export of flour from Stoate's Flour Mill. The steamship has brought bales of rags from France, which were used at that time to make paper at Watchet paper mill. Some of the bales can be seen lying on the quay (left, centre). The entrance to the harbour for ships cannot be seen in this photograph, but there was, and indeed there still is, an opening 100 feet wide this side of the lighthouse.

Watchet's busy harbour in the 1890s. A regatta is taking place and Bristol Channel pilot cutters can be seen racing outside the harbour.

Left: *Crowds of people gathered around the harbourside to witness a regatta, c.1890. The naughty man behind the beer tent is obviously unaware that he is being photographed!*

Right: *Watchet harbour after the disastrous gale of 1900.*

This steam crane, situated in the mineral railway yard, was used to load large concrete blocks for rebuilding the West Pier after the great storm of 1900.

Above: *For rebuilding the West Pier after the great gale of December 1900, tons of aggregate, shingle, sand and cement were brought to the mineral railway yard in Market Street, where it was used to make concrete blocks for the pier's reconstruction. The old mineral railway lines were still in place and were used to transport the blocks to the masons working on the pier.*

Left: *This delightful photograph, c.1903, shows the West Pier newly rebuilt in masonry and the outer part of the East Pier reconstructed in timber. Note the flatty fishing boat alongside the East Pier and the old gas lamp on the right, just visible amongst the trees.*

Quite a number of Watchet sailors in the days of sail could play either a fiddle or an accordion, usually by ear. While in port awaiting a cargo, for instance, the musical ones would often help to while away the time for all on board by playing well-known tunes. Bear in mind there was no radio or TV in those days. Posing for their photograph at Bristol in 1910 are the three-man crew of the Watchet ketch Mizpah, *three other sailors, probably from another ship, have joined them for a musical interlude.*

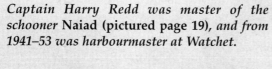

Captain Harry Redd was master of the schooner Naiad (pictured page 19), and from 1941–53 was harbourmaster at Watchet.

Left: *Captain Edmund Chidgey (master of the smack* Little Florrie).

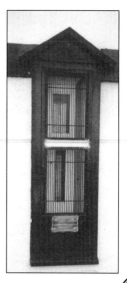

Right: *The Admiral Fitzroy barometer on Watchet Esplanade was thoughtfully presented to Watchet's seafaring community by Sir Alexander Acland-Hood, Bart, in the 1860s. It was greatly appreciated by all Watchet mariners, for at that time and indeed for many years after, it provided the only scientific help available to them in forecasting the weather. By so doing it saved many lives.*

Shipwrecks and Sorrow at Watchet

The iron schooner *Naiad*, the last Watchet-owned sailing ship, was blown ashore and wrecked at Looe, Cornwall, in 1931. Luckily all the crew were saved. Harry Redd was the master.

The *West Somerset Free Press* reported in 1889 that during the previous 24 years, 26 of Watchet's family-owned ships had been lost, and 26 sailors' lives had been taken by the cruel sea. Then followed the brief list giving the names of the lost ships, their owners and the number of men drowned in each particular ship:

Medora *(Browning and Chidgey), 3 drowned;* Trial *(R.S. Date), 4 drowned;* Providence *(Griffiths), 1 drowned;* Sisters *(Griffiths);* Laurina *(Griffiths);* Duke of Wellington *(Johnson and Case);* John *(Johnson);* John George *(J.L. Kingsbury);* Ellen *(J. Allen);* Margery *(W. Stoate);* Abeona *(R. Wedlake);* Tartar *(R. Wedlake and J. Nicholls);* Little Florrie *(E. Chidgey), 3 drowned;* Richard *(J. Short);* Union Packet *(J. Thorne);* Prudence *(G. Greenslade and J. Nurcombe);* Charles Phillips *(R.D. Case);* Rosebud *(Caroline Kingsbury);* Gannett *(T. Hall);* Princess Royal *(George Passmore), 6 drowned;* Plymouth *(R. Browning);* Betsy *(The Watchet Trading Co.);* Caroline *(J. and H. Press);* Martha *(Thos Davis), 4 drowned;* Kelso *(W. and J. Besley), 4 drowned;* Taunton Packet *(J.L. Kingsbury), 1 died of exposure.*

The following heart-breaking report in the same newspaper in April 1878 covered the loss of the smack *Little Florrie*. It was an oft-recurring story which brough great sadness to the harbour town community:

Watchet Sailors Feared Drowned

The smack Little Florrie, *belonging to Bristol and manned by a crew of Watchet sailors – Edmund Chidgey (master, aged 42), his eldest son Obed (16) and his brother-in-law William Allen – left Bridgwater on Tuesday, bound for Falmouth with a cargo of bricks. She was last spoken with by the* Thomasine and Mary *(a Watchet vessel) westward of Padstow on Thursday in the same week, and she has not since been heard of. It is feared that she has foundered and that all the hands have been drowned. Should such turn out to be the case (and there seems hardly to be a hope to the contrary) the wife of Edmund Chidgey (Rosina, of 5 Lower Folly, Watchet) loses her husband, eldest son and brother, and is left with a family of six young children. It is a most distressing case.*

Two of the surviving sons of Captain Chidgey, Alfred and Edmund junr, were forbidden thereafter to go to sea and became stonemasons. Edmund will be remembered by Watchet's elderly residents as he was a partner in the building firm Chidgey & Morse. The late Mrs Florrie Dalby, a grand-daughter of Captain Chidgey, was named Florrie after the beloved family ship.

John Short ('Yankee Jack')

The following article on John Short appeared in the *West Somerset Free Press* in 1979, written by the late Jack Hurley, a former editor of that newspaper:

Town Crier With The Golden Voice

Sailorman John Short had little or no perception of his gift... or that he was keeping a treasure trove in his head. One man was after it, and he got it... for the nation. Cecil Sharp, with the help of John Short, prince of shantymen, salvaged a national heritage of folk and sea songs that is for ever preserved in word and music. Cecil Sharp, unwearying itinerant in folk song quest, distinguished musician who devoted so many years to the collection, publication and performance of English musical treasures, chanced upon his greatest discovery when he came to West Somerset. He was tipped off to call in at Watchet, for there he could meet a happy old sailor who had long come ashore and was in the habit of reeling off sea songs as he wandered through the little town. A sailor with a golden voice to match his treasury. It was 1914, John Short was 75, and Sharp may have thought he had better hurry. But there was no need. John Short would live to 94, and go on singing almost to the day of his death. Sharp was never to forget his encounter with John, or cease to give thanks for it. For three days the two men were closeted together. In that time John Short sang more than a hundred folk songs and shanties to Sharp. A priceless outpouring, Sharp swept it into two collections for posterity. He was amazed by the extent of the old sailor's repertoire and excited beauty of his voice. John had walked the heaving decks of ships. Had destiny directed his steps differently, he might have been treading the stage of an opera house. Such was the voice of this simple-living, bearded man who wore the sailor's ample dark blue jersey and the peaked cap. But it was no use telling him. He just smiled... as always he had done when local people told him he was good. He could not understand what all the fuss was about, and he smiled again when they read to him what Cecil Sharp had written... 'John Short has, though I am sure he does not know it, very great musical ability of the uncultivated, unconscious order. His voice is rich, resonant and powerful, and yet so flexible that he can execute turns, trills and graces with a delicacy and finish that

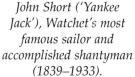

John Short ('Yankee Jack'), Watchet's most famous sailor and accomplished shantyman (1839–1933).

would excite the envy of many a professional vocalist.' The musician in Sharp could barely believe his double good fortune. Not only had he garnered one of the richest harvests in the field of song, and fulfilled his quest, beyond all expectation, he had received a bonus in pure gold of voice.

This discovery had to be shared. So Sir Richard Terry, eminent authority on the sea shanty, followed Sharp to Watchet and, listening to John Short, was enthralled. Both musicians were astonished that the voice of a man of 75 should have remained unimpaired in its quality.

John Short, born at Watchet on May 5th 1839, knew Exmoor by her frontal-falls. He sailed past those cliffs as one of many Watchet young men who shipped on the little coasting vessels. He sang as he sailed, showering liquid notes among the harsh calls of seabirds, but one day they had the show to themselves. John Short had gone into deep water. For the next 40 years he sailed... and sang. A hundred songs... to a small audience of shipmates in mid-ocean, and to listeners of many nationalities in the ports to which his deep sea voyaging took him. Privations, hardships, common to seagoing in days of sail... John sang through them all. His all-round ability as a sailor raised him to bosun; that voice of pure and powerful gold sang him into his rightful place. He was the shantyman, leader of the vocals as the canvas was crowded or shortened, anchor weighed, or the seamen went merrily round the capstan. In the 1860s John was singing on a Yankee ship in the American Civil War, and they were calling him Yankee Jack. He would slip in among his 'ton up' repertoire of sea songs one that was not... The Sweet Nightingale. It reminded him of his home port and the nightingales that sang in the groves on Cleeve Hill above Watchet's harbour. Perhaps they were calling him home. A few years before the end of the 19th century, John quit the ocean deeps and went on coasters in the Bristol Channel. Lastly, he served as mate on the Annie Christian, a Watchet-owned ship. Then, in 1900, and at the age of 61, he came ashore for good, feeling his place was by the side of his wife, whose health was failing. John's health, like his voice, was abounding, but he went no more upon the water, except to pull an oar in the harbour 'hobble' boat when the cargo steamers were berthing.

John became... of all things Town Crier! A post for which the barrack-square bawl of an ex-sergeant major would be a qualification, had fallen to the man whose voice, though powerful, was a composite of those delicate strands that had sent Cecil Sharp into ecstatics. The Town Crier appointment was in the gift of Watchet's ancient authority, the Court Leet, which still functions. It holds an annual luncheon; and to the feast, in 1931, the Court invited their Town Crier. John was then 92. So now he sang to a jury, as the Court Leet is called. Shanty upon shanty, and The Sweet Nightingale... and they marvelled, as Cecil Sharp and Sir Richard Terry had done 17 years before. Life seemed loath to let the humble sailorman go. But the last song must be sung. The long eventide John Short had been granted began to close in. On April 9th, 1933, he drew his last breath. It filled the sails of an eternal barque which carried the prince of shantymen over the horizon of time. They buried him at St Decuman's,'the kirk upon the hill' of Coleridge's Ancient Mariner. If there had to be an indisputable seal of fame upon the simple document of John Short's life, then it was supplied. He received an obituary notice in The Times! *It said of the sailor who helped salvage a treasury of song for the nation: 'He thought little of his reputation as a singer, but much more of homely things.' John Short would have liked that.*

Left: *Cecil Sharp.*
(REPRODUCED BY COURTESY OF EFDSS)

Right: *Sir Richard Terry.*

Above: *John Short with the Revd Dr Allen Brockington, of Carhampton. He introduced John to Cecil Sharp, an eminent collector of folk songs and shanties, in 1914.*

(REPRODUCED BY COURTESY OF EFDSS)

Prototype sketch of John Short ('Yankee Jack'), Watchet's most famous sailor and shantyman, by sculptor Alan Herriot. A bronze statue was commissioned by Watchet Market House Museum Society in 2007 and will be erected on the east side of the Esplanade. John was also a former Watchet Town Crier and chief of the local fire brigade.

Above, inset: *A self-portrait of Thomas Chidgey, 1855–1926. Watchet was most fortunate to have its own very talented marine artist. He was one of a family long established in the coasting trade, and went to sea at an early age. Chidgey painted the various developments of Watchet harbour during his lifetime, but his greatest joy was to paint a portrait of a ship at sea in full sail. Practically all the many sailing ships belonging to Watchet were portrayed on canvas and his ability to illustrate all the intricate rigging and sail structure of the various craft was admitted by actual sea captains. Thomas Chidgey probably never got paid very big commissions for his paintings, but painted so many because he enjoyed it and took great pride in his self-taught skill. He died in 1926 and left behind a rich heritage in his colourful record of the schooners, ketches and smacks in the last days of sail. His paintings are now much sought after and a number of them can be seen at Watchet's Market House Musuem.*

Above: *The schooner* Grimaldi *of Watchet from a painting by Thomas Chidgey. Richard Harris was owner and master from 1886–1901. Unfortunately she was wrecked in 1901 after a collison with a steamer whilst sailing from Fowey to Antwerp with a cargo of stone.*

Left: *The ketch* Friends *from a painting by Thomas Chidgey. She was owned by Captain William Norman and was severely damaged in the great storm of 1900 and sank whilst being towed to Bristol for use as a barge.*

The Gallant Little Ship With Four Names

The **Barry.**

On 24 July 1907 the newly-built paddle-steamer *Barry* called at Watchet harbour; about 100 visitors, mainly from the Welsh coast, disembarked. Over 400 passengers then embarked for an enjoyable cruise around the Holms. The *Barry* was one of the newly-formed Red Funnel Fleet, owned by the Barry Railway Company, and ran in competition against the longer estab- lished White Funnel Fleet of paddle- steamers, owned by P. & A. Campbell Ltd. After a few years of bitter rivalry the *Barry* was taken over by P. & A. Campbell. In 1911, with her funnel colour changed to white, she joined the Campbell fleet, running excursions in the Bristol Channel. In 1915, during the First World War, most Campbell ships, including the *Barry*, were commandered by HM Royal Navy and were painted grey. Because of their shallow draught, paddle-steamers were considered to be the most suitable craft for mine-sweeping. The *Barry* was sent to join the Mediterranean fleet and her name was changed to HMS *Barryfield*. With other small ships she took an active part in the ill- fated Dardanelles campaign and the Gallipoli evacuation. HMS *Barryfield* was said to be the last ship to leave Suda Bay. After the war, the *Barryfield* returned to the Bristol Channel and resumed her trips with some of the White Funnel ships which had survived the war. Her name was again changed, this time to *Waverley* – after a previous Campbell vessel of that name. In 1926, under the command of a Watchet man, Captain

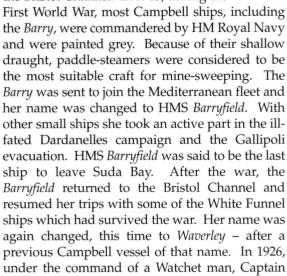

Captain William Bruford.

William Bruford, the *Waverley* left the Bristol Channel to operate from the P. & A. Campbell station at Brighton. With two other paddle-steam- ers, she ran excursions from Brighton, Eastbourne, Newhaven and Hastings, and often across the English Channel to Bologne and Calais. Another notable Watchet man who had command of a White Funnel ship was Captain Henry Chidgey. His ship, the *Glen-Avon*, was a most popular paddle- steamer in the Bristol Channel, often calling at Minehead. The commence- ment of the Second World War in 1939 saw most of the Campbell fleet, includ- ing the *Waverley*, called up once again for the dangerous task of mine-sweep- ing. The *Waverley*, again painted grey, was then given her fourth name – HMS *Snaefell*. At the evacuation of the British Expeditionary Force from the beaches of Dunkirk in 1940, HMS *Snaefell*, after embarking over 1,000 troops, was under heavy fire from German artillary. Meanwhile, another of the former Campbell ships, HMS *Glen Gower*, having rescued 1,235 soldiers, had run aground on a sandbank and was a sitting target for the German gunners. The courageous crew of HMS *Snaefell*, seeing her plight, managed with great difficulty to get a rope aboard and miraculously pulled her clear. To the great relief of the soldiers and all on board, both ships returned safely to England. Sadly, the luck of HMS *Snaefell* was to end on 5 July 1941 when that valiant little ship was bombed and sunk off Sunderland.

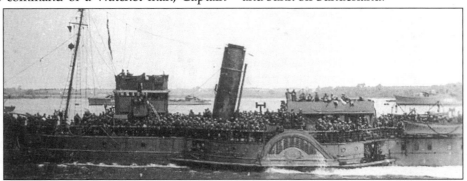

Standing room only! HMS Snaefell *(formerly the paddle-steamer* Barry*) on her return to England with over 1,000 soldiers who were evacuated from the beaches of Dunkirk in 1940.*

Ship Breaking at Watchet

Above: *A broadside view of HMS* Fox *awaiting entry into Watchet harbour, 1920.*

Right: *HMS* Fox *aground in Watchet harbour, 1920.*

On Sunday, 18 July 1920, HMS *Fox* was the largest ship ever to enter Watchet harbour. Built in 1894, this light cruiser was 336 feet in length with a beam of 50 feet, of 4,360 tons displacement and a maximum speed of 19.5 knots. For many years HMS *Fox* was one of the East Indies squadron, and her most frequent operations took place in the Persian Gulf. Here she was a powerful deterrent to gun-runners and slavers. In 1915 she assisted HMS *Goliath* to demolish enemy craft in harbour at Dar-es-Salaam, the principal port in German East Africa. By the year 1920 she was obsolete, out of commission and lying at Chatham for sale; she was purchased by the Cardiff Marine Stores Ltd to be scrapped at Watchet. She left Chatham in tow by two powerful tugs, unfortunately two days later than had been planned, and this delay was to cause problems later. Captain William Organ, a Watchet master mariner, was aboard the *Fox* in charge of operations, assisted by five Watchet sailors and three friends of the owners. Without any power-assisted steering, the Fox's steering wheel had to be turned manually, which was quite hard work for two strong men. On arrival off Watchet harbour on Sunday morning, 18 July, Captain Organ was aware that the tide had just started to ebb. Consequently, he now faced a dilemma, for there was barely enough water in the harbour for the 21 feet draught of the *Fox*. The captain also knew that the following tides would be even lower; he alone had to make a quick and serious decision. Courageously he decided to try to get the ship inside the harbour without any further delay. After detaching one of the tugs with

instructions to stand by, he ordered a wide sweep to the eastward, then, after turning to face the harbour entrance, he signalled full speed ahead to the remaining and most powerful tug. Watched by hundreds of people ashore, the great ship entered the harbour safely and, as was reported in the *West Somerset Free Press*, 'as gracefully as a yacht'. The swiftly ebbing tide, however, prevented her from laying close alongside the west pier as intended, and she grounded some 60 feet off the pier. At high water on the following tide, attempts by the tugs to push her alongside were unsuccessful. To everyone's disappointment she had to remain stranded there until Sunday, 15 August, when the tides rose high enough to enable her to be hauled alongside. On the following Tuesday, by courtesy of the ship-breaking firm, the *Fox* was open to the public for inspection. A charge for admission was made, the proceeds being kindly donated to the Watchet Nursing Association. The demolition of the *Fox* provided quite a number of jobs for local men, the work being supervised by Mr James Chapman, of Sheffield, who had previously completed the breaking up of HMS *Minotaur* at another port.

In 1923 another large ship was brought to Watchet to be scrapped – the *Dova Rio*, a beautiful 2,000-ton steel barque. She was towed into the harbour without any delay or mishap, and was duly broken up.

Because of a slump in the price of scrap metal in 1925 the Cardiff Marine Stores Ltd ceased trading. The aforementioned James Chapman decided to remain at Watchet and later became the landlord of the Bell Inn in Market Street.

Above: *The 2,000-ton steel barque* Dova Rio *being towed to Watchet in 1923 to be broken up.*

Above: *The steel barque* Dova Rio *(2,000 tons) alongside the West Pier waiting to be broken up, 1923. The remains of the cruiser* Fox *are in the foreground.*

Right: *The crew of the SS* Rushlight, *c.1952. Left to right: George ('Ginger') Jones (second mate), of Minehead, Steve Barrass (engineer), Captain Jack Allen. Fred ('Tec') Chidgey (first mate) was the photographer. Others who sailed on her included Bill Allen, Preston Ley, of Porlock Weir, and Bert Trebble ('John Bull'), of Williton.*

The ketch Charlotte, the last but one of Watchet's fleet of sailing ships, was broken up at Watchet in 1927; her master was Captain Frank Norman.

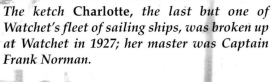

Above: *The SS* Rushlight *was a well-known Watchet steamship owned by the Wansbrough Paper Company. Built at Greenwich in 1902 and of a type known as a 'Clyde Puffer', she traded mostly from Watchet for over 40 years. During the First World War she served as a supply ship to the Grand Fleet at Scapa Flo. For most of her time at Watchet she was commanded by Captain Jim Norman, and for a few latter years by Captain Jack Allen. She ended her days at Llannelli in 1953, where she was broken up.*

Watchet Lifeboat

Watchet's first lifeboat, the Joseph Somes, *was brought by rail to Williton station in 1875, then ceremoniously hauled to Watchet by horses and launched into the harbour. The lifeboat station on Watchet's Esplanade was closed in 1944 and now serves as the public library.*

Low-water launch of the lifeboat in the 1930s.

The Harbour, A Hive of Activity

The late Alfred Harris, a very conscientious harbour maintenance man, c.1960s. After many years of faithful service to the port authority, Alfred was very reluctant indeed to retire at the age of 77.

Watchet harbourmaster Thomas Ley in the 1970s.

Mud-clearing in Watchet harbour in 1952. The mud was cleared by mechanical shovel and dumper trucks. Alfred Harris (left) and Eric Morse, standing on the stony bed of the harbour, demonstrate the height of the mud still to be shifted.

Right: *The ketch* Bonita, *of Braunton, whose master was Reuben Chichester, seen leaving Watchet harbour. In 1934 the* Bonita *was the last ship to actually sail in and out of the harbour, having no auxillary power. In August of that year she was driven ashore in a gale and wrecked at Aberthaw, South Wales. Note the black ball on the signal mast indicating to any approaching ships that there is an ample depth of water in the harbour.*

Below: *A busy Watchet harbour in 1961 with the unloading of a cargo of esparto grass for use in paper-making.*

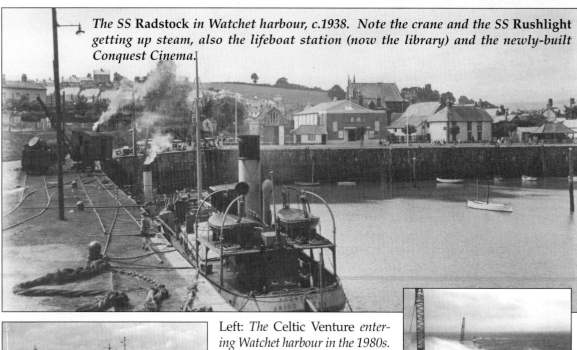

The SS **Radstock** *in Watchet harbour, c.1938. Note the crane and the SS* **Rushlight** *getting up steam, also the lifeboat station (now the library) and the newly-built Conquest Cinema.*

Left: *The* Celtic Venture *entering Watchet harbour in the 1980s.*

Right: *The East Pier being lashed by a sea driven by gale-force winds in the 1990s.*

The **William McCann**, *a small sail training vessel, entering Watchet harbour in 1985.*

Above: *Aerial view of Watchet in the late 1980s.*

Right: *Renowned yachtsman Sir Robin Knox-Johnson, who opened the Watchet Marina on 18 July 2001.*

The Ancient Mariner

Left: *The imposing statue of the Ancient Mariner on Watchet Esplanade was erected in 2003 as a tribute to Samuel Taylor Coleridge. This renowned poet composed his world-famous* Rime of the Ancient Mariner *while visiting Watchet in 1797. The statue was unveiled on 27 September 2003 by Dr Katherine Wyndham. She is pictured here, shortly after the unveiling, together with the sculptor, Alan Herriot, of Penicuik, Scotland. Sadly, Dr Katherine passed away in October 2004 at the age of 57; she died at her historic family home, Orchard Wyndham, Williton. A former lecturer at London Univerity, she gave up her career in medieval history to return to the area she had always loved. She had taken over responsibility for the 3,500-acre estate in West Somerset and a further large estate in North Wales following the death in 1982 of her father, George Colville Wyndham, a past chairman of Somerset County Council. Like her father, Dr Katherine was a great benefactor to both Watchet and Williton. Dr Katherine's mother, Anne, died in 2006, leaving two sons and a daughter.*

Some of the officers of Watchet Market House Museum Society stand proudly in front of the statue of the Ancient Mariner on Watchet Esplanade. Motivated by the Museum Committee, the statue, with the financial help of many friends, was commissioned and erected in 2003. Since then it has been very much admired by local people and thousands of visitors to the town. Left to right: Derek Quint, Jack Binding, Stephanie Franklin, Ben Norman, Roger Wedlake, Malcolm Brown.

Fishing

For many years fishing was an important part of Watchet's economy. An official report to the Admiralty in 1847 stated that '20 men were employed in fishing at Watchet with 10 flat boats and with stake nets on the foreshore.' These small, dory-type boats were known locally as flatteners or flatties, and the last ones in use at Watchet and Doniford were owned by the Besley family. They had to stop all their fishing activities in 1925 when the intense firing of anti-aircraft guns at Doniford, with the consequent falling of shrapnel, put their lives in danger. These unique flatteners were used for fishing only along the Somerset coast and on the River Parrett. Very few now exist, but a couple are preserved and on display at Watchet Boat Museum. Both shore and off-shore fishing at Watchet is still greatly enjoyed by many locals and visitors alike.

Probably one of the ugliest fish from the sea is a monkfish, which has an enormous mouth. Walter Norman caught this large specimen at Watchet and took it home on a trolley, c.1900.

Watchet Esplanade and harbour in the early 1930s. The fifth boat from the bottom is a Watchet-type fishing craft known as a flattie or flattener.

Sidney ('Dumper') Eveleigh prawning off Watchet.

Above: *John Besley, member of a great Watchet fishing family of the past. The Besley family were also manufacturers of ropes, twines and nets at the Doniford Road rope walk until the early 1930s.*

Left: *A visitor to Watchet proudly holding a large skate caught off Watchet from Shaun Anning's boat Seafire, in 2005.*

John Norman, son of Walter Norman, displays a good catch of skate, conger eel and cod which he caught in Blue Anchor Bay, c.1950s. The small boy is David Norton.

Frank Webber and his eldest sister Frances holding a conger eel caught off West Street beach, c.1948.

Clifford Beaver's conger-hunting dog among the rock pools off Watchet.

Two unknown gentlemen with a Porbeagle Shark caught in Watchet harbour in 1902.

Above: *A delighted angler proudly holds a huge cod caught from Watchet fisherman Steve Yeandle's boat* Scooby Doo Too.

Left: *Watchet angler Mark Mossman jubilantly holding a huge 26lbs 1oz cod which he caught from the shore at Minehead in 2003, then a shore record.*

Industry and Commerce

Watchet Paper Mill

Wansbrough Paper Mill, with the snow-topped Quantock Hills in the background, c.1980s.

The manufacturing of paper appears to have been a local industry for over three centuries, the earliest paper being made in 1652 on the site of the present paper mill and described as Snailholt. Paper was also being made at Egrove in 1721. John Wood, the first of four generations of that family to run the mill, took over the tenancy in 1727. Early in the nineteenth century a hymn book was published by local man Thomas Hawkes for the Methodist Church from paper made at the mill. The first paper-making machine was introduced in 1869 by the then owner, A.C. Wansbrough. In 1896 the business became a limited liability company under the style of the Wansbrough Paper Company Ltd, with Captain J.H. Wansbrough as manager; he resided at Belmont Villa. In 1898 there was a disastrous fire, resulting in much of the mill being rebuilt. Paper-bag making was also undertaken, being made both by machine and by hand. In this department the output was enormous, with bags of every description being made. In 1901 the mill was purchased by Mr W.H. Reed and it gradually expanded, new machinery being installed which resulted in increased production. In 1910 the company purchased their own steamboat, SS *Rushlight*, which made regular trips to South Wales for coal to fuel the boiler at the mill; diesel oil and gas are used to supply power today. Thousands of tons of woodpulp were imported from Scandinavia and esparto grass from Spain and North Africa, which meant employment for many men on the docks as well as revenue for the town. In 1977 the ownership once more changed hands, this time to the St Regis Group of New York. New machinery for recycling waste paper was installed. In 1871, 26 men, 23 women and 10 boys were employed at the mill. By 1900 these numbers had risen to a total of 350 being employed in paper and bag-making and by 1960 to over 500 (bag-making had then ceased). At the time of writing the number employed has plummeted to approximately 100.

Numbers 4 and 5 machines at Wansbrough Paper Mill, 1899.

Left: *Fire at Wansbrough Paper Mill, 1898. Production was lost for a considerable time whilst the mill was rebuilt. The building on the left is the iron church brought from the Brendon Hills after the closure of the iron ore mines. Known as St Saviour's Church, it was later moved to a position in West Street, now known as Greenway, and eventually scrapped.*

Below: *Group of workers at the Wansbrough Paper Mill in the late 1920s.*

Right: *A group of workmen at the Wansbrough Paper Mill in the early 1930s. Left to right, back row: ?, ?, Cecil Stone, Paddy Spence, Solomon Banks, Larnie Webber, ?; front row: ? Lewis, ? Attiwell, Napier Chubb, ?, Henry Chave, ?.*

The last work horse at Wansbrough Paper Mill, c.1953. Holding the horse's bridle is Bert Edwards.

Transport staff at the Wansbrough Paper Mill in the early 1950s. Left to right: Ivor Hole, Howard Strong, Harold Strong, John Johnstone, ?.

Left: *Howard Strong checking a lorry at Wansbrough Paper Mill in the 1970s.*

Great fire at Wansbrough Paper Mill's pulp stack, 1982. It took a week for it to be fully extinguished, during which time a smoke haze hung over Watchet.

Watchet's Superior Lime

Loading limestones into a pannier on the back of a donkey at Warren beach in 1950 shortly before the trade ended. The limestones were for burning in Warren lime-kiln.

Worthington ('Worthy') Sutton, lime burner at Warren Bay lime-kiln, c.1900. He would harness one of the lime-kiln donkeys to take him to and from his home at Bilbrook, a distance of approximately two miles.

Smeaton's lighthouse, Plymouth Hoe.

For hundreds of years, blue lias limestones from the West Somerset foreshore, extending from Stolford to Blue Anchor, were brought ashore by panniered donkeys. Mixed with culm (coal dust) the stones would be cast into the open tops of the many lime-kilns built along the coast. After hours of calcination, by means of the burning culm, the now crumbled stones would be withdrawn from the bottom of the kiln and carted away by builders or farmers. After slaking with water, builders would mix the lime with sand to make mortar, or would use it to coat the walls of cottages. In powder form lime was also much in demand by farmers whose soil was deficient in natural lime.

Watchet's hydraulic type of lime, when used as mortar, was well known for its ability to set rock-hard, even under sea water. Consequently it was much sought after by maritime engineers for the construction of docks and harbours. In 1729 John Smeaton, an eminent British engineer, ordered quantities of lime from Watchet. It was transported to Plymouth by packhorses and used in the construction of the Eddystone lighthouse. Many years later his lighthouse was superseded by a larger one, but Smeaton's lighthouse was dismantled stone by stone and re-erected on Plymouth Hoe, where it can still be seen. In 1797 William Jessop, the leading docks engineer of the entire country who had built London's West India Dock, the Ringsend Docks in Dublin and Bristol's floating harbour, considered Watchet lime to be the best in the world for building under water. As well as the lime kiln on the high cliffs at Daws Castle, Watchet had two other kilns which have long since disappeared. One was situated at the top of the slipway to the beach at West Street, the other at the lower end of Govier's Lane. The very last one to operate with the use of donkeys was at nearby Warren Bay – it was still in use in the 1950s.

The use of local lime for building came to an end when mass-produced and inexpensive Portland cement became more easily available to builders, and many farmers had found cheaper supplies of lime or changed to the use of patent fertilizers. Thus ended what was once an important local industry. With most of the kilns abandoned, they slowly disintergrated. The one in the best state of preservation today is probably at Doniford. Its production ended in the early 1900s when its slipway to the beach was washed away in a storm. The last lime burner at Doniford was Billy Binding, grandfather of Dudley Binding, Watchet's well-known and talented Morris dancer. There were many other lime-kilns alongside the Exmoor coast such as at Minehead, Porlock Weir, Lynmouth and Combe Martin. Limestones were brought to these kilns by little sailing ships from the open beaches at East Quantoxhead, Kilve or from other limestone beaches across the Bristol Channel, near Aberthaw. Supplies of culm for all the kilns were brought by sea from South Wales.

Another mineral which for many years was dug or blasted from the cliffs between Watchet and Blue Anchor was gypsum. Loaded into horse-drawn carts, it was hauled across the rocky shore to be hand-loaded into little sailing vessels which lay aground near the low water mark *(see page 39)*. Many years ago gypsum was shipped to Bristol or Swansea to be converted into plaster of Paris. Until the early 1900s many cargoes of gypsum were brought into Watchet harbour for use in the manufacture of paper at Watchet Paper Mill.

The little ships that loaded cargoes of limestone or gypsum from the open beaches often faced danger. A sudden change in the wind's direction and strength could make it difficult for them to beat off shore, and over the years a number of these craft were driven ashore and wrecked.

Left: *The ketch* Standard, *of Watchet, loading gypsum near Warren Bay at low water in the early 1900s. Note the sapling (perch) permanently fixed in the rocks, which marked the place where the vessel had to lay to avoid the rocks. Tons of gypsum were shipped from the open beach to Bristol and Swansea and used to make plaster of Paris. Some cargoes were brought into Watchet harbour and used in the manufacture of paper at the local paper mill.*

Right: *Layers of white and pink alabaster in the red cliffs between Watchet and Blue Anchor.*

Left: *Bill and Wentworth Harris's hardware shop in Anchor Street in the 1930s. Pictured are: Bill Harris, Violet Hill (sat on the motorcycle), and an unknown young lady in the sidecar.*

Below: *Watchet builder Morse and workmen at the newly-constructed Alexandra Villas, West Street, in the late 1800s. Note the old thatched cottages to the right which soon after were demolished, rebuilt and named Jubilee Terrace.*

Watchet's Department Store

W.L. Copp's dressmaking ladies at Dunster Lawns on Easter Monday 1909. Among those pictured are: M. Sparkes, Lily Williams, Lily Strong, Lanthy Morse, Lily Binding, Marie Strong, May Bale, Mary Lovell.

Watchet's only department store was run by the Copp family for several decades on premises which had been in their occupation or possession for nearly a century. It was situated in Swain Street and known as W.L. Copp & Co., General Emporium. The departments in the early 1900s consisted of general and fancy drapery, dressmaking and millinery, gentlemen's and youths' outfitting, boot and shoe wares, complete house furnishing, glass and china, general and household ironmongery. Each section of the business worked on a separate department basis, giving the public efficiency and the benefit of expert knowledge and experience. Illustrated catalogues and price lists were also available. Later the premises were divided into three separate businesses, but in August 1939 the worst fire in the business part of Watchet caused extensive damage to the building. The fire was so fierce the flames were lighting up the huge pall of black smoke in the early morning sky and at one time licking the windows of Mr Harris's shop across the lane, causing one large pane to crack. The canopy of glass covering the pavement front of the three shops was extensively damaged. The outbreak occurred in the early hours in the corner shop occupied by Miss Sully. The cause was a matter of conjecture, but believed to have been an electrical fault. The fire was attended by three brigades and among other helpers were employees of Whitelegge's fun fair which had been situated on the Esplanade during August. The three separate businesses within the premises (owned by Mrs A.G. Copp) at this time were run by Miss A.M. Sully (fruiterer, etc.), Mrs M.H. Cove (draper and furnisher), and Mr C.H. Hasnip (outfitter). On the first floor were extensive store rooms and three flats, all occupied. Immediately adjoining on one side was the newsagent's business of Mrs A.W. Sparkes, and on the other side a lane leading from Swain Street to the Esplanade, then known as Copp's Lane (now Esplanade Lane). The buildings were successfully restored and are at present occupied or owned by Evergreen Florists, Albert's Ardware Ltd, and Lloyds TSB.

At Work in Watchet

John Ennis's steam sawmills which were situated at the very top end of Govier's Lane, on the eastward side, in the 1890s. Note Portland Terrace in the background.

Part of the engineering works of John Chidgey & Sons, millwrights, wheelwrights and brass founders, etc., c.1907. John Chidgey is seated, his son Harry is on the right and the small boy is his grandson Billy Norman.

Staff of Exmoor Paper and Bag Co., c.1934. Left to right, back row: E. Spence, Dorothy Brewer, Alan Pearse, Gwen Bulpin, F. Burgess, Arthur Balmer; front row: R. MacDonald, Arthur White, Dolly Escott, Ada Griffiths, Annie Gardner, Rosie Knight, Douglas ('Buckle') Strong.

Right: Workmen of Watchet builders Chidgey & Morse in the 1920s. Note the solid tyre on the lorry. In the 1920s and '30s Chidgey & Morse undertook several building projects in Watchet, including those in Flowerdale Road (both sides) and parts of Doniford Road, Quantock Road, South Road, Wyndham Road and Whitehall.

Stoate's Flour Mill, off Anchor Street, c.1900. Workers pose for photographer Bert Hole.

The Railway

Right: *The Bristol and Exeter broad gauge railway was extended from Taunton to a terminus at Watchet in 1862. The huge locomotive pictured here has just made use of the turntable before returning to Taunton. The track was extended to Minehead 12 years later.*

Above: *Watchet station, 1870, when it was a terminus. Note the engine shed (left) and newly-built Causeway Terrace, 1859 (top left). The Methodist Church had yet to be built.*

Above: *The shunting of railway trucks by horse-power around the harbour in the 1930s was carried out by Jack Sully.*

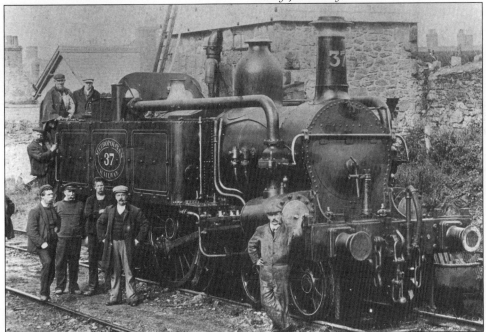

Above: *Metropolitan Railway No. 37 4–4–0. Its arrival at Watchet for the reopening of the West Somerset Mineral Railway's passenger service in 1907 caused quite a stir. A special four-truck excursion, complete with Watchet Town Band, heralded its first run from Watchet to Comberow.*

Left: *The derelict engine shed and overgrown track of the West Somerset Mineral Railway, at Whitehall, Watchet, c.1920.*

Above: *Aerial view of M. & S. Street's Transport yard, buildings and petrol pumps in South Road, c.1975. Note part of the gasometer on the left.*

Right: *Demolition of one of the gasometers in South Road, 1985.*

Right: *Binding's market (now the doctors' surgery) at The Cross in the 1920s. Above was the Cosy Cinema and ballroom.*

Below: *Date's refreshment house and shop in Swain Street, c.1910. It also displays an advertisement reading 'good accommodation for cyclists'. The proprietors, Miss Date and her sister, stand outside their quaint little shop, which seems to have bits of everything for sale. Today the attractive little building has not been greatly altered.*

Buildings and Places

St Decuman's Church

Left: *Interior of St Decuman's Church before 1886, showing the box pews and high pulpit on the right (now moved to the left and reduced in height).*

Previous to the present organ, St Decuman's was served by a small Snetzlere chamber organ (pictured right) built in 1760, which was once in Buckingham Palace. It was a birthday gift to Princess Amelia from Queen Charlotte. Eventually it came into the possession of the Earl of Egremont, whose successor, W. Wyndham, was the lay rector of St Decuman's parish. This organ was later found to be inadequate for the large choir and congregation. The matter was placed before Mr William Wyndham, of Orchard Wyndham, who offered to present the church with a new instrument at a cost of one thousand guineas. Conditional upon the gift was that the vicar preach two sermons on the Sunday nearest the feast of St Martin on behalf of the nation's poor children and that the collections on this day be divided between the Church of England Children's Society and Dr Barnardo's Homes. The new organ was built by George Osmond, of Taunton, and dedicated by the Bishop of Bath and Wells in November 1923. The 'royal' organ found its way to Eton College. Note the reredos behind the altar, which was erected in 1896 and made of Caen stone, alabaster and Derbyshire and Irish marble.

Kentsford Manor

Lying in a valley beside the Washford river, Kentsford *(above)* was the manor house of Watchet and is undoubtedly its oldest secular residence. Of two storeys with attics, the west wing may retain the plan of a late-medieval house, which appears to have been largely rebuilt c.1600. Further alterations seem to have taken place in the late-seventeenth century. A stable of about 1600 is among the farm buildings, and an old stone cross, possibly a parish boundary mark, is incorporated in a wall of the packhorse bridge. Around 1530 Sir John Luttrell sold Kentsford to Sir John Wyndham of Orchard Wyndham. His eldest son, also John, married Florence Wadham, sister of Nicholas Wadham, founder of Wadham College, Oxford. It was this Florence Wyndham who was the heroine of the well-known legend of Kentsford. The story goes that she was taken ill about a year after her marriage, and in the belief that she was dead, was buried in a vault in St Decuman's Church.

The stone cross in the foot of the wall of the packhorse bridge at Kentsford. Some say it marked the parish boundary, but its true origin remains a mystery.

During the night, knowing that some valuable rings were on her fingers, the sexton returned to the church, opened the coffin and tried remove the rings. He found the task difficult and, taking a knife, commenced to cut a finger off, but to his horror he saw blood appear and the body of the lady move. Terrified, he fled, never to be seen again, leaving his lantern behind. Florence Wyndham, now wide awake from a coma, picked up the lantern and walked down the church path and across the fields to Kentsford. Shortly afterwards she gave birth to twins, and it is said that from the son every living member of the family has descended. Similar legends are told in many parts of the country, even as near as St Audries House. The last of the family to live at Kentsford appears to have been Charles Wyndham during the reign of James II.

Following various ownerships, Kentsford was bought by the Earl of Egremont in 1806 and absorbed into the Wyndham estate.

Views of Watchet

The Ritz, Watchet's former cinema, 2005. Built by Thomas Barton Peel in Art Deco style, it was opened in 1938 by Scottish celebrity Will Fyffe under the name of the Conquest.

The newly-opened Watchet Public Hall, c.1915. It was used for many years for public meetings, silent films, concerts, pantomimes, ballroom dancing, parties, woodwork classes for boys, cookery classes for girls, etc. It was rarely used in the 1960s and was then demolished to make space for the Swain Street car park.

Above: *Interior of Watchet Community Centre, which was originally built as a British Restaurant in 1942; it had a seating capacity for 250 people. Later it was converted into a Community Centre and was a popular venue for dances, concerts, amateur dramatics, public meetings, etc. In 1960 it was converted into a garage and filling station by Mr G. Nethercott. The building was demolished in the 1980s and the site developed into a housing project now known as The Rope Walk.*

Above and below: *These cottages in Market Street, adjoining and behind the Bell Inn, were demolished in 1970 to make access for a new car park.*

Watchet Community Centre being converted into a garage, 1960.

Aftermath of the fire at the former Downfield Hotel, 2006.

Above: *The former Downfield Hotel in the 1950s. A landmark building, it was built in the late 1890s as a wedding present for a daughter of the Stoate family, staunch Methodists and owners of a once thriving flour mill which relocated from Watchet to Bristol following a devastating fire in 1911. It later became an hotel, but closed in the 1990s and the imposing Victorian building of red sandstone lay empty for a considerable time. In preparation for its re-development into apartments it was re-roofed, but sadly was gutted by fire in 2006. However, it has risen from the ruins and been rebuilt.*

Above: *A snow-blocked West Street, February 1978.*

Train pulled by 'Victor', a saddle-tank engine, steaming into Watchet station from Minehead in February 1982. This was the only means of transport in or out of Watchet at this time due to the roads being blocked by heavy snowfalls. The train managed to get as far as Williton.

Mount Pleasant (now South Road), c.1938. Victor Danby is attending his car. Note the old pound at the top of the road (now demolished).

Flowerdale Road as it was in the late 1930s. The first council-houses (on left) built in Watchet were erected in this road in the 1920s and named Flowerdale; the houses on the opposite side of the road were then called Selgrave Terrace.

Top of Liddymore Road in the late 1930s before it was given a metalled surface.

Above: *Upper Swain Street, 1905.*

Right: *Lower Swain Street in the early part of the twentieth century.*

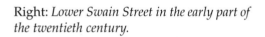

Swain Street, c.1912.

This early 1900s view of the old part of Watchet gives glimpses of a few of the town's many former industries. Bottom right is the engine shed of the old Mineral Railway at Whitehall; middle right, note the long masonry aqueduct which carried water to power Stoate's flour mill off Anchor Street. Above this can be seen a tall chimney stack, which served Thorne's steam sawmills situated near the road bridge crossing the Great Western Railway line. Mill Farmhouse (thatched), the former home of the Nicholas family, is in the centre foreground and Gliddon's iron foundry chimney stack in Swain Street is barely visible.

The upper part of West Street, 1906, showing newly-built Jubilee Terrace. Note the baker's handcart in the foreground.

Left: *View of Back River taken from the packhorse bridge in Mill Street, c.1906. The sluice gates in the foreground were at times lowered to raise and direct the river water along the mill leet, on the left; it would then turn a water-wheel to power the old corn mill further downstream.*

Malvern Road (now Doniford Road), c.1925. Severn Terrace is in the background.

Above: *An early car in West Street in the 1920s.*

Left: *Gillams Close, 2006. A new housing development in South Road, named after the field on which it was built. A row of nearby houses was named Gillam Terrace before being incorporated into St Decuman's Road.*

Personalities and Groups

Interesting Individuals

Sampling the goods of Mill Farm Dairy in the late 1930s. Left to right: Fred Doble, Dennis Pugsley, Douglas ('Buckle') Strong, Laura Nicholas, Cyril Nicholas, Reginald Williams.

Watchet chimney-sweep Frank Jones with his pony and trap outside the Parish Church at Sampford Brett, c.1930.

Well-known local journalist Will Lee, of the West Somerset Free Press, still at his desk on his 82nd birthday in 1950.

Farmer Cyril Nicholas (standing), of Mill Farm, has just supplied a churn of milk to milkman Bill Hooper (right). The young man on the motorcycle is unknown.

Geoffrey Norman, Watchet Water Company's maintenance plumber, on his motorcycle and sidebox (for tools) in Gladstone Terrace in the 1940s.

Harry Vickery, who resided at Gillam Terrace (now St Decuman's Road) and delivered greengrocery around Watchet and Williton with his horse and cart until the 1950s. He died in 1957.

Two noted councillors of Watchet – W.G. Penny (left) and W. Matthews, 1905.

Left: George Brimacombe, a well-known local character. For some years he was employed by West Somerset District Council as a roadsweeper in Watchet. In his spare time he often took part in carnivals, some as far away as Cardiff, with his roadsweeper's barrow decorated for the occasion and accompanied by his dog. He collected money for charity, for which he was awarded the BEM.

Arthur Rowe with Bizgey, c.1930s.

Arthur Rowe was a well-loved Watchet character. He was self-employed – a haulage contractor with two horses – and also the owner of a field in which he grew root crops for his animals and himself. He had a delightful and forthright way of expressing himself in local dialect. On one occasion, with his bizgey on his shoulder, he was accosted and questioned by a 'knowall' type of gentleman from London. 'Tell me, my man', he asked condescendingly, 'what do you consider to be the correct name of that implement on your shoulder?' 'It be a bizgey, zur,' replied Arthur politely. Whereupon the gentleman haughtily declared, 'Actually, my man, the precise name for that agricultural tool is a MATTOCK'. Arthur felt rather taken aback and perhaps a little rudely said: 'Thees know nort about ort, 'tis a bizgey I tell 'ee'. 'But', persisted the gent, 'can you categorically state that a bizgey, as you call it, is its authentic title?' By this time Arthur was quite irritated and testily replied, 'Corbugerdee-aye'. He then turned and angrily walked away, leaving the gent from London feeling quite bewildered. To those who might be unfamiliar with old Watchet and Williton vernacular, Arthur's final 'Corbugerdee-aye' was his exasperated local way of answering 'Yes'. In point of fact, however, unknown to Arthur at that time a bizgey was and indeed still is, just a local name for a mattock.

Right: Edmund Chidgey junr, who was a partner in the former Watchet building firm of Chidgey & Morse, builders of many housing projects in the town and district in the 1920s and '30s. He was also a former licensee of the Anchor Inn and was among the first to generate electricity in Watchet, lighting houses in Doniford Road. An application by his son, W.E.M. Chidgey, to Watchet UDC in the late 1920s to supply electricity to the town was rejected in favour of a tender from the Minehead Electricity Company.

Michael Nicholas, of Liddymore Road, winner of the cup for the best dressed front garden in Watchet, 2003.

Left: *An early photograph by James Date, c.1860s, of Henry Chidgey, ex-master mariner, landlord of the London Inn and founder of Watchet Hobblers' Association in 1863.*

Right: *On 30 May 1908 Captain Henry James Nicholas, his wife Jane (née Wedlake) and many members of this large family attended St Decuman's Church on the occasion of their golden wedding. They had 18 children.*

Dr John Moger Woolley, DL, was born in Williton in 1935, later moving with his parents, Mr and Mrs Cyril Woolley, to Watchet, where he spent his early years. His paternal grandfather was Police Sergeant F.C. Woolley, who was stationed at Williton for several years and spent his retirement there; his maternal grandfather was Edmund Chidgey, a partner in the Watchet building firm of Chidgey & Morse and also a former licensee of the Anchor Inn. Moger began his education at St Decuman's Preparatory School, Tower Hill, Williton, from where he won a scholarship to Taunton School, which he attended until 1954. From then until 1956 he completed his National Service in the Royal Artillery, becoming a second lieutenant and serving in Cyprus. On leaving the Army, he went up to the University of Bristol to read physics and graduated with a BSc in 1959. In 1975 he studied at IMEDE Business School, Lausanne.

Moger readily admits that university was his salad days and that the sports ground was his Mecca. Always keen on cricket, like his father and uncle before him, Moger, being a left-handed batsman, was a prolific run scorer. He captained the University 1st XI and also played for Somerset Seconds and club sides, always being a welcome asset to the Watchet team when available. Hockey was another of Moger's great sporting interests, and he was captain of the University 1st XI. He went on to play for both Somerset and Gloucestershire and played against England for the West in 1963. He played rugby for Somerset schools. It was during his second year at university that he met his future wife, Gill – they have a son and daughter and six grandchildren. In 1959 Moger joined E.S. & A. Robinson in Bristol as a labora-

John Moger Woolley, 2006.

tory worker and rose through the managerial ranks. A merger with John Dickinson in 1966 created a company called DRG and Moger was appointed to its board in 1979, being made chief executive in 1985. At its height DRG was a top world 500 company employing about 30,000 people, operating 167 business units in 22 countries. Its business covered engineering, packaging, stationery, papermaking and sealants. DRG was taken over in 1989 and since then Moger has been chairman of the trustees of their pension fund, which at the time of writing still has approximately 10,000 members.

From 1990–95 Moger was chairman of Dolphin Packaging plc and from 1991–98 non-executive director of Bristol Health Care Trust and Stavely Industries plc. He has been chairman of Bristol Water (Holdings) plc from 1998. Moger is a member of the Society of Merchant Venturers of Bristol, being Master from 1998–99, a member of the board of governors of Colston's Collegiate School, Bristol, and chairman of Council of the University of Bristol – the first Bristol graduate to hold the post – being a Council member since 1989. From 1997–2002 he was chairman of COTE Charity (residential care) and of BRACE (Bristol Research into Alzheimer's and Care of the Elderly). Moger was appointed a Deputy Lieutenant of Gloucestershire in 2000 and from 2002–03 was High Sheriff of Gloucestershire. In 2005 he was appointed an Honorary Doctor of Laws, University of Bristol. He is a member of the MCC and a former president of Clifton Flax Bourton Cricket Club. Outside of business, Moger's main interests besides his family are sport, travel and gardening. He lives with his wife near Winterbourne, South Gloucestershire.

Right: *Two former Watchet worthies - Richard ('Dickie') Werren (left) and Bromley Penny. 'Dickie' was surveyor to the old Urban District Council and Bromley was a local businessman and member of the Urban District Council.*

Below: *Snowballing at Watchet in the 1920s. Left to right: 'Daisy' Norman, Russell Lee, Ivor Binding, ? Tipper, Cecil Stone.*

Six naughty boys from Anchor Street caught on camera smoking woodbines on West Street beach, c.1925. The little boy second from the right is hiding his cigarette and face in shame! Left to right: Bob Harris, Walter ('Barrel') Clausen, Charlie Hunt, Howard Strong, Fred ('Tec') Chidgey, Harold Strong.

Above: *Main trophy winners at Watchet Flower Show, 1983. Left to right: Miss M. Ford (best potted plant), Mr E.C. Ayres (specimen rose), Mrs H. McDermaid (floral arrangement), Mrs D. Mayo (fruit cake and wine), Mrs S. Prole (overall runner-up in show), Carnival Queen Sallyann Nicholls, Carnival Princess Karen Yard, Kirsty Knight (overall winner of children's classes), Mr B. Lucas (vegetables and fruit cup winner), Mr E. Beaver (best onions), Mr P. House (who collected the overall winner's cup on behalf of Mr Harry Julian), Mrs Vi Bulley (best knitted garment).*

Above: *Watchet Majorettes on parade during the Watchet Carnival of 1982.*

Right: *Watchet's former Red Cross Centre celebrated its first Christmas under its new identity – the Watchet Phoenix – in 2005. This was the 17th year that the Christmas Day meal had been prepared for people who would otherwise have been on their own, and 42 meals were served. Pictured tucking into their own meals after serving the Christmas Day fare to the guests are some of the volunteers. From the left: Sheila Stenning, Joan Bosley, Ron Ridler, Jean Howe and Liz Hamshere.*

Watchet Phoenix's first year was remarkably successful under the expert guidance of seven trustees, who also form the management committee – Mrs Jean Howe (chairman), Mrs Joan Bosley (vice-chairman), Mrs Jessie Norman (minute secretary), Mrs Betty Penny (treasurer), helped by Miss Ginny Nash, Mrs Diana Bale (health and safety) and Mrs Fay Ross-Ward (fund-raising). They were appointed because they were the seven longest serving members of the Watchet Red Cross. Many

Above: *Young voluntary workers taking a break during a clean-up of St Decuman's churchyard in 1981. Top: Adrian Filer, Nick Criddle, Paul Clausen; third row: Angela Newbold, Annette Chidgey, Jill Binding, Nigel Filer, Alison Bale, Joanne White; second row: Sara Rew, Sarah Criddle, Victoria Binding, Elisa Chave, Elizabeth Bale; front row: Amanda Cooper, Helen Barnett, Jenny Sully.*

social and fund-raising events are held and there are clubs on various days when therapeutic care is regularly carried out by trained personnel. A further innovation is a computer suite. The loan of medical equipment is still carried on under the direction of Mrs Penny. Another popular function is the weekend opening of the Centre for the serving of refreshments. The Phoenix Centre is a great asset to Watchet and something to be justly proud of – long may it continue.

High Days and Holidays

Above: *A Watchet party on a charabanc outing to Cheddar Caves in the late 1920s. Seated towards the rear are Vic and Florrie Dalby.*

Right: *Mothers' Union outing to Teignmouth, 1946. Among those pictured are: Mrs Ada Jones, Mrs Cording, Mrs Caroline Stephenson, Mrs Zilla Boardman, Mrs Pickard, Mrs Maggie-May Binding, Miss Flo Peel, Revd J.L. Casserley, Mrs Violet Prole, Mrs Sully.*

Ladies of St Decuman's Church on a day trip to Cheddar, c.1920. Among those pictured are: Mrs Jack Besley, Mrs Strong, Mrs Williams, Mrs Gardner, Mrs J. Organ, Mrs Sully (Portland), Mrs E. Norman (Gladstone), Mrs 'Twist' Binding, Mrs Chidgey, Miss Evelyn Chidgey (nicknamed 'Suet Balls'), Mrs Gose Strong, Mrs V. Willicombe, Mrs Brownsey, Mrs Chidgey (Anchor Inn), Mrs Coggins, Mrs Knight (Jubilee), Mrs Prole, Mrs Langdon, Mrs Miller (Causeway), Mrs Allen (Windsor), Mrs Coles, Mrs John Norman. The driver is Mr Hill from Minehead. Note the solid tyres on the charabanc.

Watchet Schools

Non-denominational school situated beneath Watchet Methodist Chapel, c.1890. The small girl on the right is the late Mrs Polly Blackmore (née Langdon). Note the railway truck in the background.

Class 2, Watchet Council School, 1928. Left to right, back row: Ron Norman, Frank Bulley, Jack Norman, Walter Bedell, Tom Bruford, Douglas Webber; middle row: Peggy Lewis, Joan Duddridge, Florrie Webber, Ethel Morle, Phyllis Gale; front row: Henry Webber, Laurence Besley, Donald Bale, Fred Doble, Walter Webber, Ivor Attiwell.

A classroom at St Decuman's private boys' school at the Vicarage in the 1920s. The school was administered by the vicar, the Revd William Burgess (at rear).

Left: Watchet Council School, classes 5/6, 1928. Left to right, back row: Mr Harry Allen (headmaster), Bill Peppin, Bernard Date, Chris Clausen, Albert Date, Jack Binding, Fred Redd, Jack Howe, Raymond Stone, Ernie Dane; third row: Dorothy Brewer, Trixie Hunt, Vivienne Lewis, Mina Allen, Edna Norman, Phyllis Binding, Nellie Gardner, Marjorie Binding; second row: Hazel Binding, Winnie Redd, Madge Bulley, Linda Eveleigh, Dorothy Hunt, Mary Chidgey, Edna Binding; front row: Douglas Date, Ronald Burgess, Willie Watts, Dennis Leeworthy.

Watchet Council School, infants, 1928. Left to right, back row: Dorothy Stowell, Lionel Woolcott, Reg Smith, Ted Duddridge, Cyril Webber, Henry Binding, Gordon Eveleigh, Robert Binding, Clayton Morse, Kenneth Binding; third row: Vera Stevens, Phyllis Prole, Violet Leeworthy, Daisy Bale, Frances Jenkins, Gladys Langdon, Phyllis Webber, Peggy Attiwell, Mary Peppin, Blanche Diamond; second row: Rosie Binding, Jim Binding, Molly Langdon, Geva Williams, Lily Webber, Gwen Owens, Nesta Binding, Betty Pope, Peggy Bruford, Henry Cornish, Reg Cornish; front row: Kenneth Sparks, John Robottom, Leslie Prole, Fred Bishop, Ronald Coles, Ronald Binding, Edgar Norman, John Reed.

Watchet Council School middle class, c.1928. Left to right, back row: P. Wells, L. Eveleigh, B. Nicholls, W. Escott, B. Norman, D. Binding, E. Binding; third row: M. Willicombe, J. Hunt, G. Webber, M. Attiwell, B. Gardner, E. Norman, A. Thompson, B. Bond, M. Duddridge; second row: D. Taylor, W. White, R. Webber, J. Morle; front row: L. Binding, A. Williams, L. Binding, G. Williams, F. Leeworthy, A. Bishop, W. Langdon, R. Williams.

Watchet Council School percussion band at a Christmas concert in the old Public Hall in the early 1930s. Left to right, back row: *Geva Williams, Frances Jenkins, Blanche Diamond, Owen Kenyon, Kathleen Deane, Bertha Childs, Ron Binding;* middle row: *Monica Peel, Shirley Harris, Dorothy Nicholas, Alice Burgess, Roland Nicholls;* front row: *Fred Bishop, Bill Peppin, Colin Attiwell, Lilian Webber, Anka Binding, Vera Eastabrook.*

Above: *Watchet Council School in the 1950s.* Left to right, back row: *Clive Meadows, Alan Peppin, John Coggins, Roy Pardoe, Keith Stevens, Robert Gunter, David Tipper, John Jones, Robin Binding, David Wilkins;* third row: *Mr Atkinson, Helen Amery, Dorothy Langdon, Jill Chave, Margaret Watts, Sylvia Bulley, Marriane Guest, Roseanne Henry, Heather Willicombe, Sheila Jones, Veronica Bulpin, Mr T. Young (headmaster);* second row: *Jeff Barton, Margaret Bishop, June Peppin, Inga Ferrier, Jackie Woods, Priscilla Bulpin, Wendy Sully, Marion Binding, Mary House, Leonard Blackmore:* front row: *Terry Pardoe, Sidney Chilcott, John McDermaid, Ian Somerville, Jonathan Aberdein, Douglas Todd, Michael McDermaid, Peter Binding.*

Watchet Church School football team, 1952. Left to right, back row: *Norman Sully, Colin Norman, John Coombs, Gwyn Saunders, Robin Pearce;* middle row: *David Jones, David Hurley, Eric Clavey, Malcolm Bale, Graham Coggins;* front row: *Tony Sully.*

Church Life

A group of young men associated with Watchet Methodist Church in an organisation known as The Regnal League, c.1937. Left to right, seated: Pastor Alf Thompson, Victor Chubb, Harry Smith, John Reed, Reg Smith, Edgar Norman, Ted Duddridge, Jack Binding; on floor: John Mason, Bernard Date, Dennis Pugsley.

Left: The Revd David Jones, a former Watchet vicar, 1963.

The first christening at the restored St Decuman's Holy Well on 9 September 2001, when the Bishop of Taunton, the Rt Revd Andrew Radford, christened Alexander Towells. Left to right: Nathan and Ginette Towells (parents) holding Alexander, the Revd David Ireson (vicar of St Decuman's) and the Rt Revd Andrew Radford.

Right: Ringing in the New Year at St Decuman's Church tower, 1955. Left to right: Alan Pettifer, Jim Hurley, Nigel Swinburn, Cedric Bruford, Malcolm Bale, Adrian Rowe.

Left: Opening and dedication of the new Watchet cemetery, 1993. An appeal was made for donations towards the cost of trees and rose bushes which totalled £2,378. Donors could have the names of deceased loved ones inscribed on an illuminated plaque. Left to right: Dr Katherine Wyndham, Tony Knight (chairman, Watchet Town Council), Katie Knight, Alan Woodley (churchwarden), Revd Gordon Elford (Methodist), Revd Ian Mallard (Baptist), Tim Berry (Diocesan Registrar), Lieut Glyn Lewry (Salvation Army), Rt Revd Alec Hamilton (Bishop of Taunton), ?, Revd Michael Barnett (vicar of St Decuman's).

Watchet Temple Outing Club at Holford, 1908.

Left: Miss Ivy Stephenson pictured in 1988 at the console of the organ at St Decuman's Church where she was organist for 57 years; she also taught music for over 60 years. In recognition of her long service as organist she was presented with Royal Maundy Money by the Queen at Wells Cathedral in 1993, and the Royal School of Church Music awarded her an inscribed medal and certificate.

Right: The Revd William Burgess of St Decuman's Church on his James motorcycle in the early 1930s.

Right: Watchet Methodist Youth Club, 1945. Left to right, back row: Dawn Goostrey, Ruth Young, Audrey Eveleigh, ?, ?, John Hibbert; third row: Mona Date, Revd Miles, Betty Binding, Raymond Binding, ?, Muriel Young, Mrs Miles; second row: Brian Blackmore, Rex Gray, Valerie Hopkins, Shirley Stillwell, Monica Kemp, Violet James, June Williams, Helen Irving; front row: Leslie Tucker, Mollie Nicholas, Margaret Evans, Stella Binding, June Kirby, Sylvia Williams.

Watchet Law Enforcers

PS Henry Childs, c.1945.

PC Victor Newman (known locally as 'Dick Barton'), who was stationed at Watchet from 1946–54.

PC Fred Boots, c.1975.

PC Jimmy Mossman 'apprehending' his brother Alan in Watchet, c.1965.

Police at Watchet during the Second World War. Left to right: WRPC Ralph Prole, WRPC William Eveleigh, PS Henry Childs, WRPC Frank Edwards.

Left: Special Constable Nigel Swinburn, of Watchet, after receiving his long service medal in 1981.

Right: Simon Bale, Area Police Officer, 2006.

Civic Life and Working for the Community

Like many well-loved Watchet characters, Mr James was awarded a nickname, being known affectionately as 'Shippy'. He was employed by Watchet Urban District Council as a road sweeper and was well known for his amusing witticisms and Biblical quotations, which at times he used to lighten his tasks. 'Shippy' was also the Town Crier, a job which necessitated him walking around the town ringing his bell and announcing forthcoming events. During a dry, hot summer there was often a water shortage at Watchet, so to conserve supplies all the town's water was turned off at night. After announcing this, 'Shippy' would invariably add the quaint old proverb, 'You never miss the water 'til the well runs dry', followed by the time honoured cry of 'God save the King'.

William Henry James, 1936.

Before Watchet's street lighting was changed from gas to electricity he was also the street gaslamp lighter. Every evening as soon as it started to get dark, 'Shippy' would march around the town carrying a long pole with a hook on its end; this enabled him to turn on the gas tap at the top of each lamp-post. The gas would then be ignited by a small, permanently lit pilot light. 'God said let there be light' he would cry out to anyone within earshot. At about 11p.m. he would again perambulate the streets with his pole to extinguish each light in turn. On one known occasion 'Shippy's' happy lamplighting job was interrupted by some mischievious boys. Just before he had arrived to light a lamp in Gladstone Terrace the rascals had shinned up the lamp-post and blown out the pilot light. They then craftily kept well out of sight. When 'Shippy' arrived he guessed what had happened and knew he would have to fetch a ladder. To put it mildly, he was quite vexed, and it is known by one who was there that his words at that time were definitely not quotations from the Scriptures! After gas street lighting was changed to electricity in about 1927 a lamplighter was no longer required. Consequently 'Shippy's' most plaintive cry of 'Lighten our darkness we beseech Thee, O Lord', was never heard again.

'OYEZ! OYEZ! OYEZ!' The well-known cry of Town Criers around the world. In Watchet, according to the late Mr A.L. Wedlake, well-known local historian, there has probably been a crier since medieval times, selected annually by the Court Leet. An extract from the Court records of 1736 states:

Wee present Thomas Heaman to be the Common and Puplicke Cryer of the Town and Borrough of Watchet till another person to be chosen in his Room. And that no other person shall presume to exercise this office under penalty of Ten Shillings for every time that any person shall be Guilty of itt.

Richard Burton and his son Richard shared the office and that of St Decuman's Parish Clerk until 1867, when John Griffiths became the crier for the next 35 years. He liked to be known as 'John' and was the popular local barber. Having completed his apprenticeship in Bristol, he returned to Watchet, his home town, to start his own business. It is reported his voice was 'distinct and readily understood', which is often lacking in other holders of similar offices. He also served for 43 years as St Decuman's Parish Clerk.

John Short ('Yankee Jack') followed in 1902, being one of Watchet's 'all-time greats'.

Town Crier Alec Danby, 2005.

Renowned as a seaman and shantyman, he returned to nurse his ailing wife, and continued as Town Crier until 1924. Other criers followed, but details are scant except for their names – Walter ('One-eyed') Perkins, W.H. ('Shippy') James, Harry ('Tec') Chidgey, then along came Albert ('Tiddly') Strong, well remembered for notifying the town when the local water supply would be turned off. Albert worked for the old Urban District Council and then became groundsman at the Memorial Ground.

After Albert's death in the 1980s the Court Leet decided, in conjunction with the Town Council, that, with the increase in tourism, a robed Town Crier could be an asset to the town. After negotations, Alec Danby accepted the position, commencing on 1 June 1987. He has also represented Watchet not only around England and Wales, but has competed in competitions in France, Belgium, Holland, Canada, Australia and USA. Not much silverware has been brought home to date, but he did win the Ancient and Honourable Guild of Town Criers' Championship in 1990 at South Molton in Devon and the North-West of England Competition in 1998 at Sanbach, Cheshire. At the time of writing, Alec can still be seen and heard annoucing local events, being photographed, videoed and talking to the many visitors that frequent the town.

Watchet Court Leet, 1987. Left to right, standing: *Henry Dibble, Austin Burnell, Mervyn Parsons, John Hooper, Howard Strong, Alec Danby (Town Crier), Tony Knight, Harold Allen, Graham Coggins, Jack Binding (bailiff), Ben Norman, Richard Werren;* sitting: *Jimmy Hurley, Bromley Penny, Nigel Draffen (guest speaker), Michael Mills (president), George Alexander, Sidney Broomfield.*

Right: *Opening of Watchet library in 1953 by its donor, Mr L.L. Stoate. Left to right: F.P. Risdon (clerk to Watchet UDC), ?, ?, ?, A.L. Wedlake, V.E. Danby, F.B. Penny, Arthur Stoate, Dr M.D. Tonks, Mrs Tonks, L.L. Stoate, Mrs Brownsey.*

Left: *Mr F.P. Risdon holding the framed illuminated address with which he was presented to commemorate 43 years of service as clerk to Watchet Urban District Council. The address is a copy of a resolution recording the council's appreciation of Mr Risdon's services as clerk on his retirement in 1969. He was also presented with a suitably engraved silver tankard, and Mrs Risdon received a bouquet. Born in Watchet, Mr Risdon succeeded his father, Mr Frank Risdon, who was the council's first clerk in 1902. Mr J.M. Sansom was appointed the new clerk. The name of Risdon will be kept in perpetuity at Watchet by the naming of a road after it. Left to right: Mr W.H. West (chairman, Watchet UDC), Mrs Risdon, Mr F.P. Risdon, Mrs M. Sherrin (chairman, harbour committee).*

Left: *Valerie Norman with her husband Keith at Buckingham Palace after being invested with the MBE by Prince Charles in 1999. This was in recogniation of her work for charity over 20 years, during which time she raised over £100,000.*

Right: *Jean Howe after her investiture at Buckingham Palace in 1993 with the MBE for services to the community and the British Red Cross. She was also one of the prime motivators in the formation of the successful Watchet Phoenix.*

Eileen Woods was a member of the fund-raising committee to build a new Guide headquarters at Watchet. Interested in local government, Mrs Woods served on the old Watchet Urban District Council from 1967 until the formation in 1974 of Watchet Town Council, of which authority she was twice chairman. She served two periods as a Watchet representative on West Somerset District Council from 1974–91 and 1993–99, being chairman in 1982 and 1997. Mrs Woods was a governor of both the old Watchet Council School and Knights Templar School,

Eileen Woods being presented with the Guides' Thank You Badge by District Commissioner Anne Dobson, c.1970.

being chairman of the former for a period. She was also a member of Watchet Youth Club committee and the Scouts fund-raising committee. Mrs Woods was appointed to the Somerset Health Authority, serving from 1974–87, and was chairman of the Family Practitioner Committee from 1984–87. In recognition of her work for the Prince of Wales Trust she was awarded the Queen's Silver Jubilee Medal in 1977, and was invested with the MBE in 1983 in recognition of her services to the community.

William Challice was born at Cannington in 1888 and the only education he received was at the village school. He left school before he was 14 and started work in the garden of a large local house. The life of a gardener did not appeal to him and after a few months he left this employment and became apprenticed to a carpenter. At the age of 20 he obtained employment at his trade at Paxton, near Weston-super-Mare, and three months later got a job in Bristol. After two years in that city he began to think seriously of trying for the Police Force. He first made application for Bristol City Force, but on going under the height standard he was threequarters of an inch too short. Not discouraged, he undertook a correspondence course of stretching movements designed to increase height. On completion of the course he applied at Bristol Police, but was then found to be still a quarter of an inch too short, so was not accepted. After this he tried to join various police forces, again without success. Still determined to join the Police, he again applied to the Metropolitan Force, this time with success, and was told to report on 15 November, 1910. After completing 11 years of service he was promoted to sergeant and later to station sergeant. He was then promoted to the rank of inspector after 19 years of service. William Challice retired from the Metropolitan Police in 1937 at the age of 48 after 26 years of service. He decided to return to Somerset and settled in his wife's home town at

William Challice in his early twenties.

Watchet. On the outbreak of the Second World War he was recalled by the Metropolitan Police, but after a few months was released into retirement again. On his return to Watchet he joined a first aid party and in due course took charge of it. He took over driving an ambulance, a voluntary job in those days, and became a member of St John Ambulance Brigade in 1941. He was superintendent of the Watchet Division during the 1940s and 1950s and undertook ambulance transport in the area on a full-time basis. Watchet became one of the recognised small country stations and Mr Challice personally gave a 24-hour service from 1948 onwards. His ambulance was always at the ready and he did all the driving. When the ambulance was not in use he spent his time cleaning and maintaining it – all on a voluntary basis. As a result of his commitment to the St John Ambulance Brigade Mr Challice was awarded the British Empire Medal (no longer awarded) in 1955 and later the same year was admitted to the Order of St John of Jerusalem in the grade of serving brother, his investiture taking place in 1956. On approaching the age of 70 he decided to give up after completing 15 years' service in St John and over 10 years driving ambulances. Mr Challice was also a member of Watchet Urban District Council and the local Court Leet. He was much respected and had a great sense of humour. He died in 1981 at the age of 93.

Local Hunts

Meet of West Somerset Foxhounds in the courtyard of the West Somerset Hotel, Watchet, 1912.

Meet of otter hounds at Watchet railway station, c.1920.

Remembering the War

Watchet Home Guard at camp on the Brendon Hills, 1943. Left to right, back row: *Stan Duddridge, Jimmy Lee, Arthur Tudball, Percy Williams, Ron Prole, Bill Sully, ?, Jack Goostrey, Les Kirby;* middle row: *Len Eveleigh, Frank Warren, Stan Amies, Tom Bulpin, Bill Watts, Jack Clavey, James Bryant;* front row: *Edgar Norman, George Willicombe, Victor Danby, Harry Bulpin, Joe Hunt, Basil Bindon.*

Enjoying a drink at the Watchet Royal British Legion Club in the 1950s. **Among those standing are:** *Blanche Alexander, Gordon Eveleigh, Jack Reed, Albert Bale, Redfers Willicombe, Frank Webber, Bill Wells, Des Chubb, Alfie Edwards; sitting: Joe Bale and Ernest Jones.*

Above: *Watchet Royal British Legion Band leading the parade up Swain Street in commemoration of the 50th anniversary of VE Day, May 1995.*

Left: *Second World War veterans' parade in commemoration of the 50th anniversary of VJ Day, August 1995.*

Below: *Ex-servicemen enjoying a well-earned pint after the 50th anniversary VJ Day parade, August 1995. Left to right: Ben Norman, Malcolm Brown, Ron Purcell, Jack Martin, Robert Hornby, Gerald Putt. Seated in the wheelchair is Fred Doble.*

Watchet Royal British Legion

Watchet Royal British Legion Band in its formation year, 1952. Left to right, back row: Ted Alexander, Jack Alexander, Tony Bruford, John Taylor, David Wilson, Brian Tucker, Tom Bowden, Norman Sully, Peter Wilson, Alf Short, Alf Jones, Philip Jones, John Coombs, Jock Burke, Fred Trunks; front row: Rodney Wells, Barry Date.

Watchet Royal British Legion Band, 2006. Left to right, back row: Lee Watson, Kathleen Maun, Chris Bashford, Dennis Smith, Colin Whitworth, Michael Justice, Peter Owen, Peter Wilson, Bob Coles, John Coombs, Niall Watson, David Parkman, Richard Binding; front row: Jenny Robins, Jodie Brown, Dave Tilling (musical director), Claire Whitworth, Melanie Hooper.

Watchet Salvation Army Corps

Watchet Salvation Army Corps, 1907.

In the journal of the West Somerset Village History Society, 2005, Mr Chris Saunders researched and listed the names and locations of quite a number of former Watchet public houses which had ceased trading many years ago. His list includes the White Hart, which was situated at 27 Market Street (now the home of Mr Fred Bacon). In 1882 a new branch of the Salvation Army was formed at Watchet and the former pub was purchased for use as their first meeting place. General Booth's name appears on the title deeds, together with a covenant preventing future use of the building for the sale of alcohol. It is recorded that the first attempt to form a Corps at Watchet was made at that time by Captain Rice Nurcombe; he linked up with Mr F.A. Cockram and Mr Bob Chubb. These three, wearing bright red jerseys, held an open-air meeting at the harbour slipway, and then marched up Swain Street loudly singing 'You must be a lover of the Lord'. It was at No. 27 Market Street that Watchet's first Salvationists were converted. Among them was George Langdon, a young lad who was destined to spend his whole life in the service of the Salvation Army, eventually rising to the high rank of Commissioner. By 1884, 27 Market Street was too small to accommodate the many new recruits who had joined the ranks. Fortunately at that time the former Methodist Chapel in Swain Street became available and was taken over as the headquarters of Watchet Corps No. 570. The names of the first officers appointed at the time were Captain Castle and Lieutenant Hall. From that time onward the building was referred to as Castle Hall. On Sundays, attired in smart military-style uniforms, the Salvationists marched to hold open-air services in many parts of the town. The singing of 'Onward Christian Soldiers' and other rousing hymns, accompanied by their excellent brass band, was greatly enjoyed by many townsfolk and visitors. Encouraged by this response, the Corps decided to hold a trial open-air service at Minehead. According to a long-deceased Salvationist who was there as a youth, the Minehead meeting was a disaster. 'The officers, choristers and bandsmen,' he said, 'were disgracefully heckled and booed by some misguided youths.' They returned very disappointed to Watchet where their music and good deeds were always appreciated. Many years later on 15 December 1928, Watchet's Salvationists proudly opened their very own newly-built Citadel, which had been financed mainly by their own efforts. To everyone's joy, it was ceremoniously declared open by the aforementioned Watchet lad, Commissioner George Langdon. The Citadel, situated in a prominent position overlooking the railway and the town's main street, is a welcoming building and a credit to all concerned.

Watchet Salvation Army Band, 1931. Wilfred Bale is on the far right, sitting.

73

Entertainment and Performance

Trevor Martin, who was well known in Watchet, being an enthusiastic worker for the Town Band, West Somerset Railway and the Methodist Church. He died in 2006.

Watchet piper Fred Bacon serenading the town from the west pier, 2005.

Above: *Dorothy Bond's Orchestra, c.1930s. Left to right: Joe Buncombe, Archie Davis, Stan Coggins, Dorothy Bond.*

Right: *Four members of Watchet Town Band in the 1920s. Left to right: William Knight senr, Harold Prole, Henry Chave, William Knight junr.*

Watchet Town Band celebrating their 110th year in 2003. Left to right, back row: Chris Crockford, Dennis Bulpin, Randolph Bulpin, Adrian Rowe, Michael Prescott, David Wilkins, Ruth Austin, Mark Tranter, Jodie Cooke, Bob Izzard, Matthew Cooke, Audrey Manning, Roy Chave; front row: Elizabeth Manning, Arthur Pye, Jenny Perkins, Geoff Perkins, Richard Binding, Ron Turner, Heather Crockford.

Concert party organised by the Revd William Burgess, c.1920. Left to right, back row: *Bill Gardner, Marjorie Martin, Bill Martin, Ivy Stephenson, Jack Bowden, Phyllis Hunt, Cory Hole, Avis Peel, Cecily Stephens;* middle row: *Jim Hurley, Alice Sully, Beatie Peppin, Bessie Bond, Nora Bale, Gwen Vickery, Jack Brownsey;* front row: *Dick Bulpin.*

Watchet Ladies' Conservative Club's presentation of The Butterfly Queen *in 1929.* Left to right, back row: *Phyllis Gale, Russell Norman, Annabel Lee, Rita Morse (bridegroom), Phyllis Hunt, Ivy Stephenson (bride), Sid Hooper, Edna Binding;* third row: *Ethel Morle, Joan Richards, Howard Strong, Gladys Coggins, Tom Pearce, Madge Bulley, May Watts, Walter Allen, Sylvia Gay, Ena Strong;* second row: *Joyce Danby, Madge Attiwell, ? Bindon, Phyllis Bond, ? Stevens, ?, ?, Brenda Bond, Margaret Chidgey, Frances Jenkinson, ?, ? Stevens, Gwen Lloyd, Peggy Lewis, Dorothy Hunt, Betty Yandle;* front row: *?, Fred Chidgey, Daisy Bale, Muriel Jones.*

Above: *Some of the cast in Watchet British Legion's production of* Ali Baba and the Forty Thieves *in the Town Hall, 1933.* Left to right: *John Norman, Walter ('Dan Leno') Binding, Fred ('Titcher') Chidgey, Eileen Morgan, Bessie Bond, Eva Norman, Ronald Prole, Ernest Nicholls, Vic Dalby.*

Right: *Amateur dramatics at the Community Centre in the 1950s.* Left to right: *?, Bob Eaton, Maggie Binding, Ron Mayo, June Williams, ?, Marjorie Miles, Leslie Wedlake, ?.*

Cast of Jack and the Beanstalk *performed at the old Public Hall, c.1939.* Left to right, back row: *Beryl Bulpin, Joyce Hill, Alma Lloyd, Dennis Langdon, Pamela Davis, Phyllis Stephens, Peggy Milton, Bert Lloyd, Vera Eastabrook, Rose Nicholas, Jim Nicholas, Glyn Evans, Walter ('Dan Leno') Binding, Edna Stephens, Hector Binding, Jean Allen, Mavis Conway, Thelma Davis;* front row: *June Kirby, Delphine Morgan, Margaret Sully, Iris Milton, Josy Knipe, Maureen Knipe.*

Watchet Women's Institute

Watchet WI banner, made in 1950 to a design by Mr Sutherland Reed, husband of a member. The cross pole was carved by Mr E. Willicombe and the embroidery was carried out by members, whose names appear on its reverse.

Diana Bale, president (left) and Jane Butland, maker of the cake to celebrate the 75th anniversary of Watchet's Women's Institute in 2004.

Watchet Women's Institute celebrate their 75th anniversary in 2004. Among the guests were twins Betty Madge and Peggy Norton, who joined the Institute when they were just 14, each having clocked up 70 years as members. Left to right, standing: Peggy Wheel, Mavis Bryant, Joyce Dunn, Ann Binding, Janet Martin, Jacqui Hampton, Diana Bale, Ethel Kirby, Joan Morris, June Roberts, Peggy Norton, Jane Butland, Jessie Norman; seated: Maidie Ford, Betty Madge.

Watchet's Cubs, Brownies, Guides and Sea Scouts

Above: *Watchet Cubs on the Esplanade, c.1958. Left to right: Margaret Bale, Tony Knight, Roger Groves (holding flag), Michael Higgins, John Duddridge, Trevor Yates, John Putt, David Bulley, Richard Burnell, ?, John Nicholas, Noel Taylor, Roy Chave, ?, Alan Stephenson, John Trunks, Margaret Smart, Richard Werren, Vi Knight.*

Below: *A Mastermind quiz between 1st Watchet Brownies and 1st Watchet Cubs in 1981 resulted in a win for the Brownies. Left to right, back row: Nicola Barbour, Caroline Reynolds, Elisa Chave, Alison Pope, Lisa Chidgey, Stacey Lillington, Susan Wells, Marie Giles, Karen Amery, Samantha Lawrence, Emma Reed, Martine Hooper, Margaret Pye; middle row: Glenda Bale, Andrew Sumpter, Keith Jones, Chris Phillingham, Jason Musson, Simon Bale; bottom row: Marion Noble, ?, ?, ?, Matthew Mozeley, ?, Paul Clavey, Bernice Danby, Marion Fry.*

Above: *Jenny Sully heading the Watchet contingent of the Girl Guides at the St George's Day parade at Dunster, c.1988.*

Right: *Girl Guides at a Scout Jamboree at Nettlecombe Court, c.1952. Left to right, back row: Elaine Morgan, Laureen Prole, Daphne Pullin, Janet Western, ?; front row: Christine Langdon, Madge Dalby, Sylvia Gulliford, ?.*

Below: *Watchet Sea Scouts under scoutmaster John Norman. The Admiralty tug* Haldane *alongside the West Pier was used as a safety vessel in connection with the gunnery range at Doniford and target-towing aeroplanes in the 1930s.*

In 1728 the distinguished author Daniel Defoe, during his many journeys around Britain, visited Watchet. Defoe was not very impressed with Watchet's harbour, which he considered was built too low and with insufficient length to adequately shelter shipping. He was quite impressed, however, with the local lime-burning industry, but was completely mystified on seeing the fossils on the fore-shore. He wrote as follows (note the Old English spellings):

Daniel Defoe, c.1728.

From hence the Coaft bears back Eaft to Watchet, a fmall Port of late Years, tho' formerly much more confiderable; for it had given Place to Minehead, tho' now it is in a much better Condition than it us'd to be in: And this it owes to two Acts of Parliament; one pafs'd in the 6th Year of th late Queen Anne, for repairing of its Quay and Harbour; and the other in the 10th. But when the Works defigned were near completed, it was found, that the Quay was built much too low, and not extended to a fufficient Length to preferve the Town, and the Ships and Veffels riding in the Harbour, from the Violence of the Sea: Whereupon another Act paffed, in the 7th of King George I for continuing the Duties laid by the former Acts, and remedying the Inconveniencies before mentioned. It feems to me, that the Town of Minehead rofe out of the Decay of the Towns of Porlock and Watchet.

On this Coaft are vaft Quantities of Rock, or rather Pebble, which the sea, at low Water, leaves uncovered; from whence the neighbouring Inhabitants fetch them on Shore to an higher Ground, and burn them into Lime, for dreff-ing their Land; but it is more efpecially ufeful in Building; as no Cement whatfoever is more lafting for Jets d'Eaux, Heads, Piers, and other Mafonry, that is to lie under water; in which Pofition it runs up to a Stone as hard as Marble. The Cliffs are ftored with Alabafter, which, by the Wafh of the Sea, falls down, and is conveyed from hence to Briftol, and other Places on this Shore, in great Plenty. Neither fhould it be omitted, that the Inhabitants burn great Quantities of Sea-weed, to fupply the Glafs makers at Briftol.

Walking on the Beach near Watchet, I difcov-ered among the large Gravel great Number of Stones, fluted in Imitation of the Shells of Fifhes of all Kinds. Many of the flat Kind are double, and curioufly tallied one in another, which may, by a violent Stroke, be feparated. How to account for the vaft Variety to be found here of this Sport of Nature. I know not: Some I have feen as broad of a Pewter-difh, and again others no bigger than a Pepper-corn; but in all of them the Flutings are regular; fome like the fcalop, in Rays from a Centre; others like the Periwinkle, in fpiral Lines: In thefe, and all other Form, they lie here in great Plenty.

Fossils on Watchet's and Doniford's rocky foreshores can still be found and are sought after by visitors, espe-cially children. Perhaps with its colourful red cliffs, layered with pink and white alabaster, and the many little rock pools in which small crabs and prawns can be caught, Watchet's rocky beaches offer a thought-provoking alternative to a featureless sandy beach. On display in Watchet Market House Museum is a very interesting collection of local fossils. These include a very fine ichtyosaurus, some huge mammoths' teeth, many varied ammonites, devil's toenails (coiled oysters) and marine snails. The Museum is open daily during the summer.

Sport and Leisure

Mixed Bathing at Watchet 100 Years Ago

A James Date photograph showing a swimming-pool which was manually excavated at Helwell Bay in the late 1800s.

This photograph by James Date shows the railway carriage (left) *which was used as a changing-room for lady bathers at Helwell Bay in the late 1800s.*

Until the late 1800s sea bathing along the Somerset coast was not particularly popular. With the arrival of the railway, however, many visitors to Weston-super-Mare, Minehead and Watchet started to take a dip in the briny. Doctors by this time were recommending it as a healthy exercise. Nevertheless, many puritanical people considered mixed sex bathing to be undesirable, and to see women undressing on the beach, to them, was really quite shocking. At Weston and Minehead this problem was solved by providing bathing machines (huts on wheels), which were moved up and down a section of the beach reserved for females only. After changing into their bathing costumes, ladies could discreetly enter the water without attracting undue attention or offending any shy gentlemen who happened to glance in their direction.

The rocky beaches at Watchet were unsuitable for bathing machines but, as at Minehead, enthusiastic townsfolk were keen to provide facilities and welcome bathers. Helwell Bay was considered Watchet's most suitable place for ladies' bathing. With great ingenuity, a small, redundant railway passenger carriage was set up for the use of ladies at the inner corner of the bay. Minus its wheels, it was positioned on a ledge, near the bottom of the cliff, with wooden steps providing access from the top of the cliff and down to the beach below. Bathing at Helwell Bay,

West Street beach, c.1915.

however, was practicable for only two hours each side of high water. To remedy this a large bathing-pool, five feet in depth, was manually excavated on a nearby rocky part of the beach. Sad to relate, but with hindsight not surprisingly, both of these ambitious enterprises were doomed to failure. Watchet's enemy of old, one 'Davy Jones', constantly filled the laboriously dug-out bathing-pool with sand and stones, and keeping it clear proved to be a losing battle. The same infamous old sea devil Jones also caused huge waves from the north-east to undermine the soft marl cliffs of the bay. After a while, to everyone's dismay, the ingenious ladies' changing-rooms collapsed onto the beach.

Some years later, in 1907, Watchet's Town Councillors received complaints that shameless women had again been seen changing on the beach at Helwell Bay and bathing with members of the opposite sex! After discussing the matter the Council decided to erect a flight of wooden steps at the inner corner of the bay. A changing-tent for females only was made available on the recreation-ground above, which at that time was owned by the Council. It would be superintended by a Mrs Bulpin, who was permitted to make a small charge for its use. The Councillors hoped that 'Mixed sex bathing could in future take place at Watchet with modesty and decorum'. How times have changed!

Beachside Fun

The bathing platform at Helwell Bay was always very popular with young people learning to swim. This happy group in the 1930s are waiting for the tide to come in. Standing, top: Peggy Milton; left to right, sitting: Eileen Norman, Evelyn Bruford, Gwen Bulpin, ?, ?; standing: Henry Binding, Dicky Hill, ?; sitting on sand: ?, Peggy Bruford.

Bathers enjoying the water at Helwell Bay in the 1930s.

Cricket

Watchet Cricket Club First XI, 1933. Left to right, back row: C. Langdon (umpire), T. Pennington, J. Howe, S. Cutler, A. Strong; front row: A.J. Ricketts, H. Gimblett (three years later Harold was playing for England at Lord's), A.W. ('Jimmy') Hurley, F.B. Penny, W. Branchflower, R. Stone, C. Hooper.

Watchet Cricket 1st XI, 1953. Left to right, back row: J. Denman (umpire), Desmond Chubb, Chris Milton, Clifford Milton, Trevor Strong, Fred Doble; front row: Bromley Penny (secretary), Alfie Edwards, Gerald Stevens, Alan Pearse (captain), Jack Binding, Arthur Ricketts, Colin Sansom, Hedley Stevens (scorer).

Watchet Cricket Club tour based at Leicester, 1948. Left to right, back row: P. Hutchings, P.J. Barnes, A. Edwards, A.A. Pearse, L.E. Withers, H.O. Isaac, C.H. Martin, G. Stevens, C.T. Hann, F.B. Penny; middle row: R.A. Jennings, W.J. Barnes, E.W. Farmer, D.J.Barnes, R.C. Ireland; front row: E.J. Binding, P.P. Leach, H.R. Gladwell, A.J. Ricketts.

Haydn ('Tanner') Sully, a former Watchet cricketer who went on to play for both Somerset and Northamptonshire, was born at Sampford Brett where he spent his early years before moving to Watchet. His father was a well-known figure there, not only for delivering goods from the railway by a horse-drawn dray but also as a sportsman. Despite the handicap of a childhood illness, Haydn won a scholarship to Huish's Grammar School in Taunton. He displayed cricketing talent from an early age and his right-arm off-spin bowling and left-hand batting earned him a place in the Watchet Colts team, from where he progressed to play regularly for the 2nd XI. Before he played many games for the senior team, his skills with both bat and ball brought him to the attention of the Somerset coach of the time, Bill Andrews, and the Watchet youngster joined the playing staff at the County Ground at Taunton. Haydn made his first-class debut for Somerset in 1959, but with the likes of Brian Langford already well established on the staff,

Haydn Sully.

his opportunities with his native county were always going to be limited. Over the next four seasons he played a dozen games for Somerset, during which he took 12 wickets, his best return being 5-64. Realising that he would have to change counties to play regular first team cricket, Haydn joined Northamptonshire in 1964 and plied his trade there for the next six seasons with considerable success. In 1966, his first full season with his newly-adopted county, he took 101 wickets at an average of 21.21. During his time with Northants, Haydn played in 110 championship matches, taking 302 wickets, including one hat-trick, before leaving in 1969. He went on to play Minor Counties cricket for Devon and captained club side Sidmouth. Outside of cricket, Haydn had a successful career working for Whiteways Cyder, going on to become a director with Showering Vine Products before he retired. Before his death in 2006 at the age of 67, Haydn resided with his wife Margarett at Honiton, Devon.

Left: *Barbara Strong, who has helped prepare and serve teas at home matches for Watchet Cricket Club for over 50 years. She has deservedly been made an honorary life member of the club.*

Right: *Andy Milton receiving Watchet Cricket Club's Player of the Year trophy for 1981 from Somerset player Dennis Breakwell.*

Watchet Cricket Club social evening, 1980. Left to right, standing: *Pat Binding, Hilde Nicholas, Joyce Milton, Raymond Clavey, Margaret Axon, Pam Clavey, Barry Suchley, Barbara Strong;* seated: *Mo Parsons, Joyce Gibbins, Pat Munson, Betty Setterfield.*

Challenge cricket match at Watchet, 2005 – David Milton's XI v. P. Milton's XI. Left to right, back row: *Andrew Woodward, Andrew Martin, Liam Woolgrove, Chris Sully, Chris Wookey, Ben Saddington, Adam Bishop, Aaron Deeks, Jamie Milton, Callum Knight, Dominic Bowden, Nigel Merrick, Philip Bowden, Stephen Waterman, Fred Powis, Warren Knight, Andy Pyne, Matthew Bowden, Paul Clavey, Edward Martin;* front row: *Tayler Maddocks, Edward Owen, John Harris, Phillip Milton, David Milton, David Knight, Ryan Strong, Philip Sylvester, Jason Strong;* on ground: *Martin Strong.*

Football

Left: *Watchet Rovers Football team, 1907–08. Before the War Memorial Ground was established in 1926, footballers made use of the ground adjacent to and above Helwell Bay which was known as the Recreation Ground.* Left to right, back row: *Ernest Binding, C. Nicholas (referee), Bill Groves, Bob Lovell, W. Carruthers, Edmond Woods, Percy Fort, Joe Harris, Charlie Webber:* front row: *Fred Chidgey, Alf Strong, Fred Attiwell, Ralph Chidgey, Ern Binding.*

Watchet Reserves, West Somerset League Division II champions, 1930–31. Left to right, back row: *Albert Strong (trainer), Arthur Sully, Albert Chave, Percy Clavey, Jack Chidgey ('Bristol Jack');* middle row: *Harold Allen, Wally Knight, Charlie Short;* front row: *Reg Chave, R. Ruddick, George Perkins, Dennis Norman, Bill Gunney ('Wooller').*

Right: *Watchet Town Football Club, 1939–40.* Left to right, back row: *Fred Bishop, W. Gardner, Jack Bulpin, Arthur Langdon, Walt ('Barrel') Clausen, Raymond Stone, ? Chidgey;* middle row: *Arthur Sully, Hector Tuckfield, Alan Pearse, ?;* front row: *Dennis Pugsley, Bob Chilcott, George Alexander, Russell Norman, Fred Doble;* insets: *Jack Burge, Donald Hawkes, John Cubitt.*

Watchet Casuals, 1945–46. Left to right, back row: Brian Kemp, Trevor Willicombe, John Willicombe, Trevor Hunt, Mervyn Parsons, Donald Webber, John Lee; front row: Raymond Clavey, Frank Webber, Owen Binding, John Kirby, Mr W.R. ('Crickey') Chidgey (manager), Raymond Binding, Alec Mayo, Glanmore Robottom, Tony West.

Watchet Colts, 1947–48. Left to right, back row: Mr Ernie Binding (manager), Eric Binding, Geoff Griffin, Ray Odam, Danny Bryan, Pat Edwards, Donald Webber, Raymond Clavey, Mr Guy Sadler; front row: Glyn Willicombe, Billy Sherlock, Geoff Day, Frank Webber, John Lee, Chris Milton, Trevor Webber.

Watchet Town AFC, 1951–52. Left to right, back row: ? Blackmore, ? Griffin, Arthur Mayo, Alf Bishop, Dennis Williams, Des Chubb, Philip Toogood, Jack Clavey, Ray Odam, Trevor Strong, Clifford Milton, Ron Prole, ? Hunt, Tom Husband, Jack Yates, Ernie Dane; front row: Edwin ('Spiv') Stevens, Les Stevens, Frank Webber, Ray Binding, Alfie Edwards, George Whiteman, George Alexander, Ronnie West, Pat West; on ground: Harry Husband, Michael Clausen (mascot), Tony West.

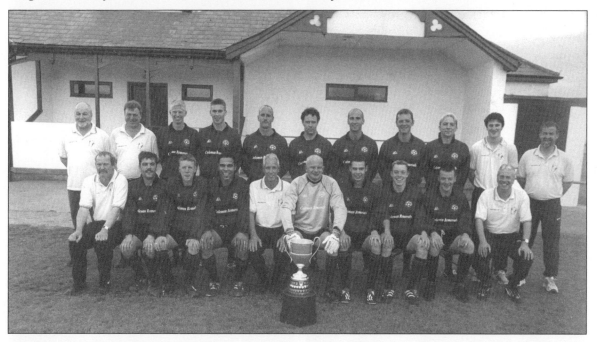

Watchet Town Football Club, Somerset Senior Cup winners, 2001–02. Left to right, back row: Stuart Norman (treasurer), Mike Stout (linesman), Wayne Merrick, Gary Trunks, Dave Spence, Steve Wild, Dean Allen, Nick Criddle, Mike Jones, Ben Saddington, Robin Saddington (physio); front row: David Knight (football secretary), Mark Clausen, Matt Knowles, Paul Raymond, Pete Cowling (chairman), Steve Moore, Andrew Woodward, John Harris, Lawrence Monaghan, Nick Sully (manager). Prior to this, Watchet last won the Somerset Senior Cup in the season 1958–59. Founded in 1887 and playing their first matches in a field near St Decuman's Church, Watchet Town FC have rigidly adhered to their familiar red and black shirts since 1893–94. Previous to that there were no regular colours with players wearing shirts according to their fancy. In season 1939–40 Watchet entertained a team of ten professionals and one amateur from Doniford Army Camp, which included Reg Lewis and Alf Kirchin of Arsenal and Sep Smith of Leicester City. Watchet hammered the visitors 6–1 and this was rated by many as their finest game.

Skittles

Watchet Red and Blacks Ladies' Skittles Team, c.1981. Left to right, back row: Mo Parsons, Joyce Gibbins, Dave Ruddy (sticker-up), Hilde Nicholas, Lin Strong; front row: Marilyn Binding, Debbie Watts, Christine Bendle.

Watchet Upstarts skittles team, winners of the Bridgwater Rugby Club's Knock-out Cup, 1985. Left to right, back row: Cliff Milton, Roy Williams, Alan Hutchins, Tony Pendry; front row: Nigel Bray, Philip Watts, Geoff Vaulter.

Presentation evening for Bell All Stars skittlers, 1994. This was a unique season for the team as they were Division A champions and winners of the Front Pin, Alan Clarke and Landlords' cups. Left to right, back row: Geoff Vaulter, Richard Owens, Richard Binding, Alan Hutchins, Stuart Walker (sticker-up), Mike Axon, Mike Higgins, Keith Strong; front row: Robert Greenslade, Jimmy Nicholas, Roy Williams, Adrian Griffiths.

Watchet's Foreign Legion Ladies' skittles group displaying their trophies in 1989. Left to right, back row: Joyce Owens, Chris Allen, Pam Perkins, Bridget Jones, Janet Waterman, Eve Perkins; front row: Diane Allen, Denise McLaren, Sandra Holness.

Horses

Alfred Gardner (left) with his horse Tom, adjudged to have been the best dressed horse in the Watchet Horse Show which took place on the Recreation Ground in 1910.

First, second and third prizewinners at Watchet horse parade, 1911.

Other Sports and Pastimes

Watchet and Williton Cycling Club, c.1890s.

BALLOON ASCENT: WATCHET.   AUG. BANKHOLIDAY. -/08.

Before 1903, no-one had ever seen or flown in an areoplane. The only way to get into the air at that time was by means of a large balloon, inflated by hot air or gas. The first balloon flight to be seen in West Somerset took place at Watchet in 1908 and thousands of people gathered on the Recreation Ground to see Miss Spencer Kavanagh, a daring young lady, take to the air. She was strapped into a parachute beneath a huge balloon, which had been inflated with gas from the local gasworks. Fervent prayers for her safety were led by the local vicar; then, at the appointed time, amid thunderous applause from the crowd, Miss Kavanagh slowly ascended into the air and drifted away. Later everyone was pleased to hear that the brave young lady had landed safely at Egrove Farm, about two miles distant as the crow – or balloon – flies.

Left: *Famous athlete Gordon Pirie signing autographs at the AA championship sports at Watchet Memorial Ground, 1954.*

Above: *Some Watchet Amateur Boxing Club members ('the Old Uns') since its inception in 1953. Left to right, back row: C. Norman, D. Lewis, J. Perkins, N. Allen, C. Milton, R. Bendon, P. Jones, T. Stout, A. Stout; front row: F. Kirby, G. Perkins, F. Collinson.*

Right: *Watchet's Helen McDermaid, winner of the Somerset Champion of Champions Bowls Cup, 1991.*

Watchet Bowling Club, who won the coveted Turnbull Cup for the first time in their 94-year history in 2005 and retained it in 2006. Left to right, back row: W. Strong, A. Taylor, J. Hooper, N. Williams, A. Rendell, R. Somerfield, I. Trunks, J. Trunks, R. Rendell; middle row: S. Slade, P. Tregidgo, M. Webber, M. McDermaid (president), F. Webber, D. Fowkes, R. Wells; front row: C. Bruford (captain), G. Vaulter, K. Bulpin, C. Williams, D. Davis, A. Bryant.

Carnival

Young entrants in Watchet's 1928 Carnival. Left to right: Fred Fish **(parcel),** Gordon Neal **(rabbit),** Philip Toogood **(Red Indian),** Ben Norman **(Channel swimmer).**

Master Reg Smith, aged six, with his much-envied custom-built sports car with person-alised number plate. He took first prize in Watchet Children's Carnival in 1928.

Right: *Muriel ('Mo') and Tony ('Jacker') Sully dressed for entry in Watchet Carnival, c.1947.*

This hearty group cycled from Minehead to Watchet raising funds on the way for the re-starting of Watchet Carnival in 1976. Among the cyclists are: Ray Walters, Colin Northam, Les Munson, Roger Sylvester. *Standing on the right are:* Tommy Perkins *and* Bernice Danby.

Left: *Watchet Mothers' Club with their winning Cries of London entry in the club section of the 1977 Watchet Carnival. Among those pictured are: Liz Lillington, Josephine Sheppard, Jenny Taylor, Helen Rawle, Stella Blunt, Sue Brereton.*

Right: *St Decuman's Parish Wives' winning entry of Tulips from Amsterdam in the 1978 Watchet Carnival. Left to right: June Phillingham, Pat Binding, Iris Champion, Valerie Webber, Joyce Chidgey, Molly Willicombe, Joyce Spoor, Yvonne Swinburn.*

2nd Watchet Brownies Marmite entry in the 2002 Watchet Carnival. Left to right, back row: Joyce Chidgey, Lisa Chidgey, Claire Wright; front row: Georgia Perkins, Laura Kemmish, Samantha Greer, Becky Riggs, Stephanie Williams, Beth Rogers.

Watchet 1000

Replica Viking longboats land during the Watchet 1000 celebrations in 1988.

In 1988, to commemorate Watchet's 1,000 years of history since its invasion by the Vikings, many of the town's organisations set up events to mark the occasion. Perhaps the most spectacular was staged by Watchet Boat Owners, who built and manned two replica Viking longboats. With horns in their helmets, the rascals sailed into the harbour to reinact the raid on Watchet Mint. The Mint was unsuccessfully defended by a large number of ancient Britons and Saxons (a role assumed by the sea scouts). The Vikings then rowed away with their illgotten gains, including several innocent Watchet damsels.

Watchet's Court Leet still meets once a year at the Bell Inn where many years ago it administered crude justice to Watchet's wrong-doers. To take part in the Watchet 1000 events, the Court held two open-air sessions on the Esplanade. On each occasion the dignified officers of the Court were disturbed and insulted by rude women who, dressed as witches, were seen and heard casting spells. They were in turn arrested by the constables of the Court and, after a fair trial, were found guilty. After being strapped into the Court's ancient ducking stool, each one was emersed in the harbour six times. After subsequent enquires the names of the witches were revealed as Jessie Norman, Fiona Chidgey and Valerie Mainwaring.

Fighting for 'equal rights for women' during the Watchet 1000 celebrations in 1988. Left to right: Jessie Norman, Margaret Norman, Diane Coggins.

Carrying the witch to the ducking stool at Watchet 1000 celebrations in 1988. Left to right: Howard Strong, Robin Turner, John Danby, Valerie Norman (witch), Ben Norman.

Chapter 3

WILLITON

Agriculture and Commerce

On The Farm

Early picture of farming at Williton, c.1890.

Harvest scene at Williton, 1936. Fred ('Boxhat') Bulpin is on the binder and Fred Spence is holding the horses' reins. Also pictured are: Redvers Besley, Len Webber, Vigar Langdon, Walter Chilcott, Arthur and Ray Cavill.

Astride a Ferguson tractor at Bridge Farm, c.1950s. Left to right: Paul Gliddon, Ruth Gliddon, Richard Gliddon, Brian Veale, Roy Williams, Peter White.

Roy Williams and Chris Parbery enjoying their lunch break in a Bridge Farm field, with a Ferguson tractor behind them, c.1950s.

Bill Parker, Harry Towells and Aubrey Hill collecting new Massey Ferguson tractors from J. Gliddon & Sons at Williton for work at Huish Barton Farm, c.1960.

Enjoying a break at Bridge Farm, c.1950s. Left to right: David Biggs, Art Cavill, Chris Parbery.

Bill Pugsley (driving a Ferguson tractor) with Roy Williams drilling corn in a Bridge Farm field, c.1950s.

Ken Stephens combining a Bridge Farm field in 1968.

Night-time Dutch barn blaze at Bridge Farm, Williton, October 2002.

Right: *The Bridge Farm Dutch barn with straw still burning two days after the blaze in 2002. Some 80 tons of straw were destroyed, also four vehicles; the total cost of the damage was estimated at £500,000. The barn was later demolished.*

Dairy and Livestock

Albert E. Bulpin, of the former Beaconwood Dairy.

Frank Holcombe (left), Stan Paviour and George Milton at Beaconwood Dairy on the corner of Wyndham Terrace and Bridge Street, c.1940s.

An old Beaconwood Dairy milk bottle.

Above: *Sheep heading towards Bridge Farm from Bridge Street in the 1930s.*

Left: *Ayrshire herd of cows at Bridge Farm, 1950. Farmer Ronald Gliddon and herdsman Percy Long are in the background* (right).

Butchers and Bakers

Bullock outside Williton Meat Supply, c.1958. Left to right: John Barber, Sid Holcombe, Philip Webber, Bill Pugsley, Fred Hutchings (proprietor).

Williton Meat Supply, c.1970s. Left to right: Bill Pugsley, Fred Hutchings (proprietor), Sid Holcombe, Philip Webber.

Williton Meat Supply staff enjoy a cuppa, c.1970s. Left to right: Arthur Hillier, Les Bleaker, Mark Munslow, Garnet Hopkins, Bill Pugsley.

Above: Baker Sam Jones's family, 1934. Left to right, back: Arthur, Lloyd, Norman; front row; Betty, Sam, Mrs Sam Jones.

Above: *An early-twentieth-century view of W.H Jones & Sons baker's shop with Horner's grocery and draper's shop on the extreme left and the boys standing in the doorway of Langdon's butcher's shop. The pony and trap seen in North Street was used by Jones's for delivering bread.*

Right: *Edwin ('Nobby') Boyles delivering bread for Langdon & Sons' Steam Bakery, c.1910. The bakery was situated at the bottom of Long Street, opposite the Railway Hotel (now the Foresters Hotel).*

Grocery Stores

At the turn of the last century the site on which now stands The County Stores and J. Jones & Son was occupied by shops specialising in groceries, drapery, men's outfitting, ironmongery and general hardware. They were run by Mr W.E. Gallop, who had two assistants, Mr T.W. Hann and Mr E.C. Parsons. These assistants eventually rose, by the time of the First World War, to being in a position to buy the business.

As Parsons & Hann, it further developed the grocery side, with an extensive country round by the end of the war. They were at that time the main grocers in Williton. The gentlemen's outfitters was continued with the late Maurice Bryne giving long service in that department. In 1929

Gallop's grocery, household goods, drapery, men's outfitting and ironmongery store at the turn of the last century. It later became Parsons & Hann and is now the County Stores and J. Jones & Son, greengrocers and florists.

Mr Claude Hann, elder son of Mr T.W. Hann, having qualified as a chemist, opened a dispensary and general pharmacy section on the premises. They were the first chemists Williton had ever had.

By the early 1930s Parsons & Hann had reached almost department store status with furnishing and drapery and a sweet and tobacco department. Horse-drawn vans of the Gallop days had long since given way to Ford vans, well known throughout West Somerset.

Mr E.C. Parsons and Mr T.W. Hann died within a year of each other, the latter in 1941, the former in 1942, the business then continuing under Mr Claude Hann and his younger brother, Mr Hedley Hann. In 1962 the premises were leased to The County Stores, of Taunton, and they bought the building in 1973. In May 1976 the old building was demolished because of irreparable damage when a car and lorry struck it, rocking the foundations and disturbing the ancient beams. New premises were built, comprising a shop on the ground floor and four flats above. The new supermarket was officially opened in November, 1976.

Above: *One of the founder-members of Parsons & Hann* (left) *with his family* (from left) *Theodore William Hann, Claude Hann, Hedley Hann, Mrs Augusta Hann.*

Left: *From the Watchet Urban Council's Official Guide of Watchet and Williton, 1907.*

Management and staff of Parsons & Hann off on their annual outing, c.1920s. Hedley Hann is standing in the centre with cap.

Parsons & Hann (now The County Stores) decorated to celebrate the Coronation of King George VI, 1937.

Clockmakers

James Thristle III, c.1870.

Clock and jeweller's shop at Bellamy's Corner in the early 1900s, with a Thristle clock mounted on the wall.

In the nineteenth century three generations of the Thristle family were quite famous local clockmakers. One of the best known was James Thristle II, who was born in Stogursey in 1802. Having completed his training with his father, he moved to Williton to set up a clockmaking business. His house and shop was on the corner of High Street and Bank Street; this was demolished in 1938 for road widening. It is now an open space adjoining the NatWest Bank. He later resided at Priest House (where the Church Room now stands) and also owned a property called Escott House in Long Street and land at Highbridge, later building four cottages. James Thristle II supplied the clock for the Shire Hall in Taunton early in the nineteenth century, and the Thristles looked after clocks at Dunster Castle, St Audries House and Orchard Wyndham. In 1823 he married Mary Honiball, from which union came a son, Thomas, who was not interested in following his father's trade. He became a maltster and brewer at Bristol, later becoming landlord of the Plume of Feathers, Minehead. Whereas James II had no son to help him in the business, his brother Joseph had two sons, James III and Francis. James III moved to Williton to work with his uncle, with the arrangement that there would be an informed partnership between the two of them. This is confirmed by the clocks signed James Thristle and Nephew. In 1862 James Thristle III married Betty Hirst, of Digley, Yorkshire; she died in 1875, aged 48 years. James II died in 1877. In 1898 Henry Hardin succeeded the Thristle family in the clockmaking and jewellery business at Williton and he in turn was succeeded by Tom Bellamy, after whom Bellamy's Corner is so named. Many Thristle clocks are still in use today and quite sought after; one is on display at Watchet Market House Museum.

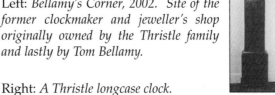

Left: *Bellamy's Corner, 2002. Site of the former clockmaker and jeweller's shop originally owned by the Thristle family and lastly by Tom Bellamy.*

Right: *A Thristle longcase clock.*

Other Shops and Businesses

Above: *Aftermath of a fire at Williton Sawmills, near the railway station, in 1919.*

Left: *Herbert H. Hole's photography shop in Long Street, c.1900.*

In January 2004 more than half a century of family history came to an end when Ben Gliddon retired from the well-known and long-standing Williton family-run business of J. Gliddon & Sons. He first began working for the Gliddon's agricultural, engineering and garage business during his school holidays. In 1959 he joined the company payroll and began learning the various aspects of the business with guidance from his father Laity.

Sadly just six years later his father died suddenly at the age of 57 and Ben found himself in charge of the garage. He also managed to find time to help his uncle John with the agricultural side of the business until his cousin David joined the family firm in the early 1960s.

Ben Gliddon is pictured in the centre with his wife Margaret and cousin David on the forecourt of the Williton garage.

Ben's favourite leisure time activity is golf, being a former captain of the Minehead and West Somerset Club. Margaret, his wife, is a daughter of the late Mr and Mrs H.J. Chibbett, another old Williton name with business connections. Her father was principal of the former local building firm, J. Chibbett & Sons, and her mother was an organist at St Peter's Church for many years and a prominent member and past president of Williton Women's Institute. Gliddons disposed of the garage side of their business in February, 2004.

Buildings and Places

Views of Williton

*An artist's impression
of Williton from Lines
in the 1850s.*

This picture: *Bridge Street, c.1912.*
Below left: *The cottages on the left (Bridge Street) have long since been demolished.*
Below right: *Bridge Street, Williton, c.1930.*

Fore Street, Williton, c.1905.

Fore Street, Williton, in the late 1940s.

Above: *Williton Rural District Council offices in the course of erection in Fore Street, 1937. They were opened in January, 1938, by Mr A.F. Luttrell, the architect being Mr R.E. Jackman and the builder Mr W.E. Dewar, of Minehead.*

Above: *Architect's design of the new West Somerset Council offices in the course of erection at Killick Way, Williton, at the time of writing.*

North Street, c.1910.

The old St Peter's School Lane, which now leads to St Peter's Close. The former school buildings in the background are used as offices for Magna Housing Association, 2002.

Half Acre in Edwardian times.

From a painting of Long Street in Victorian times.

Coronation decorations in Long Street to celebrate the crowning of George V, 1911.

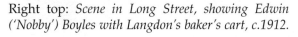

Right top: *Scene in Long Street, showing Edwin ('Nobby') Boyles with Langdon's baker's cart, c.1912.*

Right, middle: *The Wyndham estate house and office (now Croftways) near the Recreation Ground entrance in Long Street, c.1920.*

Right: *Top of Long Street in the late 1920s, showing Bradbeer's Garage in the background.*

Dwellings

Above: *Townsend Cottages at the top of Limpetshell Lane, c.1900. Eliza Chilcott stands beside her daughter Annis outside their cottage.*

Left: *Magnolia House, Long Street, c.1900.*

Two cottages destroyed by fire at Highbridge, Williton, 1928. The cottages were occupied by Mr E. Brooks and Mr C. Holcombe. Williton Fire Brigade turned out, but had to push their engine to the scene as no horses were available. Their services were not required as the Minehead brigade got there in 20 minutes and had everything well in hand. This caused a certain amount of ridicule to be heaped on the Williton brigade.

The former Williton Union Workhouse in 2006 after its multi-million pound restoration and conversion into 37 homes and 17 flats by Bristol-based Platinum Developments UK Ltd. Now named Sir Gilbert Scott Court after its designer, the old workhouse was ready for occupation in 1838 following the 1834 Poor Law Amendment Act. Its construction cost £6,000 and had places for 300 paupers. The universal dread of the workhouse and its conditions are still remembered by older folk (see Jack Hurley's Rattle His Bones*). The system survived almost without change until the birth of the National Health Service in 1948 when the workhouse became the Williton and District Hospital for the Aged. In 1989 it was replaced by a purpose-built hospital at what is now called Shutgate Meadow. The old buildings became unsafe and the grounds unsightly and the restoration has breathed a new lease of life into the site.*

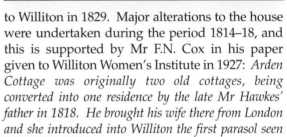

Right: *The Victorian parterre with box hedges at Highbridge House, adjacent to Williton railway station, 2002.*

Situated in Long Street, Arden Cottage is one of the oldest dwellings in Williton, being built in the fourteenth century or possibly earlier. Although named a cottage, it appears now as a long, thatched two-storey house with a north-west wing. Paul Upton, in a paper which appeared in the Journal of the West Somerset Village History Society, No. 30, 2005, states that Arden Cottage is probably a 'romantic name given to the house in the nineteenth century' and the building is clearly a house, not a cottage. It is a cruck-framed house, originally of three bays, with a further two bays added to the west. The roof trusses and rafters are smoke-blackened from the times when the fire was in the middle of the house. A house of this size and date would indicate that the owner was of some importance – possibly a yeoman farmer with a number of servants and workers.

Arden Cottage.

The house probably pre-dated the naming of Long Street in 1472–73 and was, perhaps, one of several farms to the east of Williton. Certainly, Long Street was not a thoroughfare until the Bridgwater to Minehead turnpike road was improved by a cut from West Quantoxhead direct

to Williton in 1829. Major alterations to the house were undertaken during the period 1814–18, and this is supported by Mr F.N. Cox in his paper given to Williton Women's Institute in 1927: *Arden Cottage was originally two old cottages, being converted into one residence by the late Mr Hawkes' father in 1818. He brought his wife there from London and she introduced into Williton the first parasol seen in the village.*

The Wyndham estate sold many of its properties, including Arden Cottage, in the twentieth century. It was bought by Mr Edwin Henry Morris from Doniford for £990 in 1920. He died in 1924 and the property was sold to the Misses Eleanor Beatrice Whyte and Esme Whyte. In 1934 it was sold to the Westminster Bank, who was trustee for the will of the late husband of Violet Cairns, who owned the property until her death in 1955. It was then bought by Lt-Col R.G. Archer, who lived there until the Misses Geach and Willcocks bought it in 1961. They ran it as a bed and breakfast and Miss Geach became well known locally as a water-colourist. Mr Upton bought Arden Cottage in 2003, since when he has carried out major restoration work.

Dovetons and the Egremont Hotel

Left: *Dovetons (also known as The Limes), minus the lime trees, 2002.*

Below: *Dovetons (also known as The Limes), Long Street, showing the lime trees (removed in the 1960s), which were reputed to have been over 500 years old, c.1910.*

Egremont Hotel, c.1920s. The remains of the ancient cross pictured standing at the corner of the Egremont Hotel can now be seen preserved in the garden by the NatWest Bank.

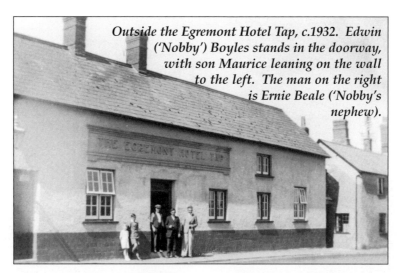

Outside the Egremont Hotel Tap, c.1932. Edwin ('Nobby') Boyles stands in the doorway, with son Maurice leaning on the wall to the left. The man on the right is Ernie Beale ('Nobby's nephew).

Probably the earliest known inn in Williton was the Blue Anchor, a fifteenth-century ale house on the site of the former Egremont Hotel. From there it became the Coach and Horses Inn, a centre for stagecoach activity in the early-eighteenth century when it was increased in size to include three letting bedrooms and provide a second façade around the corner into Bank Street. In those days the coaches used to drive through an opening between Gliddon's shop and the hotel (almost opposite what is now the NatWest Bank) into the cobbled yard at the rear of the building. It was also a centre for the administration of law with police courts being held there. In 1830 the final enlargement created the hotel as it was lastly known, being extended to adjoin Gliddon's shop and providing an additional seven bedrooms, a ballroom, ground floor public rooms and the kitchens, which replaced some of the stables. Also added was the Egremont Hotel Tap on the site occupied in 2007 by an estate agent and hair salon. It was originally named the Wyndham Hotel, but became the Egremont Hotel in 1842. The Egremont Hotel closed in January 2003 and it

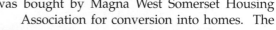

The former Egremont Hotel after its conversion into apartments in 2004.

was bought by Magna West Somerset Housing Association for conversion into homes. The elevations and façade of the Grade II listed building have not been altered and during the building renovations at least one treasure was discovered when an original cooking range built by Williton firm J. Gliddon & Sons was found behind panelling and was not allowed to be removed. Some of the stables at the rear of the building have been preserved and others sympathetically converted. Thus brought to an end the building's 600 years as an hostelry.

Egremont Court from the stable yard, 2004.

Left: *The old kitchen range discovered in a wall on the first floor during the redevelopment of the former Egremont Hotel in 2003. The room was probably servants' quarters. The late-nineteenth-century range is inscribed with the name J. Gliddon & Sons, Williton, and is intact even with a baking tin still in the oven. Mr David Gliddon, a descendant of the firm of installers of the range, wanted to remove and resite it at his Stogumber home, but his request was turned down by West Somerset District Council, who said it represented the removal of historic fabric from the Grade II listed building. An old Gliddon's kitchen range was also discovered during renovations at the Bell Inn, Watchet.*

Other Landmarks

Above: *The old Williton fire station, 1992, where the library now stands in Killick Way. This fire station was built in 1938 by J. Chibbett & Sons. It was demolished in 1993 after a new fire station was built in North Road. The Station Officer in 1938 was Arthur Holcombe, followed by C. Lyddon, C. Shopland, W. Symonds, D. Howells, D.W. Sully MBE, and R. Chamberlain.*

Above: *This sign, originally erected in 1925, was removed from outside the New Inn (now the Royal Huntsman) after the outbreak of the Second World War in 1939 for fear it would be of help to the enemy in the event of a German invasion. It was found in the Old Mill at Yarde many years later.*

Below: *The old West Somerset Free Press works in North Street, where the newspaper was printed every week without a break for 129 years. The last issue to be printed there rolled off the presses in November, 1989. The paper is now printed at Plymouth, but is still compiled at Williton.*

Right: *Last British Rail train at Williton, 2 January 1971.*
Left to right: *Gordon Hudson, Tim Pearce, Roger Risdon.*

BBC West Regional broadcasting station (now the Tropiquaria) at Washford Cross; it was built in 1933. When being erected, one of the masts fell down, resulting in fatalities.

Patrick Cook, artist, collector and author, was brought up in Bristol and worked in London for some 20 years. He returned to the West Country about 11 years ago to open the Bakelite Museum, which is situated near St Peter's Church.

The mill, by the River Willite (which becomes the River Swill at its mouth at Doniford), dates from the 1780s and replaced one built on the same site over 100 years earlier. The last miller there was Reg Sutton, who ground wheat, barley, oats, maize and beans until the mid-1960s. The old water-wheel is still in position and a rural history collection can also be seen on the top floor of the mill.

BBC TV's Flog It *presenter Paul Martin (left) and Patrick Cook outside the Bakelite Museum at Orchard Mill, Williton, in 2005.*

Patrick became interested in Bakelite at an early age and the first item he purchased was a Bakelite wireless in 1968 costing £5 (quite expensive for those days). Since then his Bakelite and plastic collection has expanded to become one of the largest in the country, spanning the history of plastics from 1850 to the present. In 1907 a Belgian chemist, Dr Leo Baekeland, working in New York, first invented synthetic plastic by using resin. A petrol derivative, its name is phenol formaldehyde. When mixed with pigments, catalysts and woodflour as a filler the resin could be moulded under extreme heat and pressure to produce a strong, stable and very resistant plastic. True Bakelite – the name orginates from the inventor's surname – could only be produced in black or brown because of the woodfiller until 1920 when clear and many bright colours were introduced.

Originally, Bakelite was an expensive and fashionable material, allowing designers to work in bold, geometric forms producing a considerable quantity of various household commodities – egg cups, lamps, telephones, wirelesses, toys, etc. – in a range of colours and Art Deco shapes; also cars and bicycles. The largest mouldings made were coffins, but these were not a great success as they are not biogradable for use in burials and could not be used for cremations. After the Second World War, Bakelite fell from consumers' favour for a considerable time.

The Bakelite Museum has been featured in media programmes such as *Flog It*, *Bargain Hunt* and *Collectors' Lot*, also holiday programmes and on Radio 4. The museum is open from Easter to the end of September and well worth a visit. For the older visitor it is a trip down memory lane.

Sir Alexander Acland-Hood's victory parade through Williton after the 1906 General Election.

Clifford Tarr (left) standing beside an Austin A40 pick-up truck and David Bulpin beside an A40 van, c.1960s.

Left: Sir Alexander Peregrine Fuller Acland-Hood, Bt., 2nd Lord St Audries, at the opening of the new ATC Hall at Williton in 1966. Flanking him are Air Commodore Betts, OC Locking (left) and F/Lt Ron Slade (right).

Right: Dudley Ward (Liberal), seated in the rear of the car with hat, being greeted by supporters at Williton during an election tour, 1911.

Norman James Jones ran the Williton Bakery for 30 years after taking it over from his father and uncle in 1960. He was president of the Master Bakers' Association in 1983 and at the end of his term of office was made an honorary life member. He was born and brought up in Williton, starting his education at St Peter's School and then proceeding to Minehead County (later Grammar) School. In the late 1930s he moved to Dorset and was appointed master at Shaftesbury Workhouse.

Norman James Jones wearing his presidential chain of office of the Master Bakers' Association.

After serving for six years in the Queen's Own Dorset Yeomanry during the Second World War, Norman joined the family bakery firm at Williton. Here he continued the bakery's Christmas tradition of roasting turkeys in the large bread ovens for Williton folk.

Norman was a man of both foresight and determination who argued his point forcefully and bore no malice.

He spent 13 years as Squadron Leader of 1013 Quantock Squadron ATC, and died in 1996, aged 78 years.

Personalities and Groups

Individuals of Note

The late G.B. ('Mac') Mattravers, who was a well-known driver with Bryant's Coaches for many years.

Sid Holcombe, of The Court, North Street (now The Square). Born mentally retarded, Sid became an inmate of the Union Workhouse after the death of his mother. He was well known and liked in the village and had the uncanny knack to be the first to know when a circus was to visit Williton. When asked the time he would always reply 'Appatoo' (half-past two)!

Clifford ('Teet') Bryant, a former well-known character of Williton and Watchet.

Left: The late Reg Braunton, a true gentleman of Williton.

Below: Budding Williton cricketers, c.1965. Left to right: David Cooke, John Clarke, Nicholas Sully, Stuart Chidgey, Chris Coles, Philip Wilkinson.

Frank Percival Risdon was born at Watchet, the son of Mr and Mrs Frank Risdon, who later resided at Williton. He was educated at Clifton College, won the Cook's Law Prize, and after a year in London joined his father in Risdon & Co., solicitors. In 1934 he married Miss Eileen Beattie from Minehead and they had two children, Roger and Jan.

On the death of his father in 1958 he became the senior partner in the firm until his retirement in 1974. His knowledge and interest in local government were invaluable and he was an excellent administrator. He had succeeded his father as clerk to the Watchet Urban District Council and to the Williton Rural District Council, relinquishing these posts in 1969 having served at Watchet for 43 years and at Williton for 37 years. He was one of the original sub-commissioners of pilotage when the Watchet

Frank Percival Risdon.

Pilotage District was set up in 1936.

During the Second World War he was evacuation officer, food executive officer and local fuel overseer. He was a founder-member of the League of Friends of Williton Hospital, and for many years was the superintendent registrar for the District of Exmoor.

Mr Risdon had an interest in all games, but the love of his sporting life was lawn tennis and for 19 years he played for Somerset in the singles. For a similar length of time he was secretary and treasurer of the County Association, and was a former president of the county. The Minehead Lawn Tennis Club owed much to his support and enthusiam, and the Prudential County Championships were held at Minehead for nearly 20 years as a result of this. Mr Risdon died at his home, Stoneytrows, Williton, in 1986, aged 82.

Peter R. Swann, BSc, PhD, was born at Williton in 1935, spending most of his early years at his grandmother's (Mrs Elizabeth Duddridge) home in Doniford Road. He says he has fond memories of all the years he spent at his grandmother's, who was an exceptional lady and set a good standard for his brother Rex and himself. He remembers well Mrs Bulpin and Mr Jack Chilcott, the blind basket-maker, spending many hours watching him work his magic turning the withies into perfectly formed baskets.

He began his education at St Peter's School, Williton, in 1939, moving on to Caldecott Road School, Camberwell, London, in 1944. He then attended Dulwich College from 1946–53, the University of Wales from 1953–56 where he gained a BSc, University of Alberta, Canada, 1956–57, and Cambridge University 1957–60, where he gained a PhD.

Peter became a scientist, the idea of which he first fancied at the age of 16, but spent almost all his working life abroad, starting his own company in the USA making scientific instruments. His younger brother Rex joined him in the venture, looking after the manufacturing side. They proceeded to have a research laboratory in California and a manufacturing base in Pittsburgh. Quite suddenly in 1990 Peter and his brother decided to sell their jointly-owned business, which they did in two stages – 70 per cent for 35 million dollars, then the remaining 30 per cent for 50 million dollars, making 85 million dollars in all.

Peter R. Swann.

Peter built a house on Jumby Bay Island (*see page 149*), in which he now resides and named it Doniford House after the happy times spent on Doniford beach in his boyhood.

Positions he has held include senior scientist, US Steel Corporation; visiting professor, University of Goetingen, Germany; CEGB Professor of Materials Science, University of London; co-founder and president of Gatan Inc.; and chairman of the Jumby Bay Island Company, Antigua. Honours Peter has achieved include Rhodesian Selection Trust Award to study copper production in Zambia; Gilbert Foyle travel award to visit metallurgical facilities in USA and Canada, Robert Lansing Hardy Gold Medal – AIME young scientist award; Campbell Award – NACE award for research on the mechanisms stress corrosion failure; ASTM first prize in metallography; Sheffield Metallurgical Society prize for contributions to metallurgical research; Swedish Metallography Award for work on the structure of iron silicon alloys; Beilby Gold Medal and Prize of the Royal Chemical Society and Institute of Metals; conducted California Symphony Orchestra; Microscopy Society of America, 1997 and Distinguished Scientist Award in Physical Sciences. Peter has also produced over 53 publications, 25 technical notes and patents in the field of metallurgy, materials science and electron microscopy.

Above: *Interior of Mrs Tavener's refreshment hut and shop on the roadside at Liddymore, c.1925. Mrs Tavener opened the shop to supply refreshments and oddments to Territorial Army troops when they spent their summer camp at Liddymore. In the ensuing years many Williton children found it a welcome haven on the way back from the beach at Doniford. Mrs Tavener also had a shop in Swain Street, Watchet.* Left to right: *Miss Winnie Knight, Mrs Tavener, Miss Organ.*

Right: *Barrister Kate Chidgey, 2006, eldest daughter of Stuart and Anne Chidgey, formerly of Williton, and a grand-daughter of Vera Chidgey, of Williton, and the late Jack Chidgey, who was a member of a well-known former Williton family. Kate was educated at Blundell's School, Tiverton, and Oxford University, where she obtained a BA Honours degree. On leaving Oxford she attended City University and BPP Law School, London, and was called to the Bar of the Inner Temple in 2006. Kate practises in criminal law.*

Above: *Bob Gibson* (left) *and Tony Williams removed this giant bees' honeycomb from inside one of the roofs of the Egremont Hotel whilst working for J. Chibbett & Sons, c.1970.*

Left: *The late Mrs Kathleen Winter celebrated her 100th birthday in November, 2004. She had resided in Williton for over 65 years, being the widow of Chris Winter, who was also well known locally. Kathleen, holding her birthday greeting from the Queen, is pictured with her daughter Jenny.*

John F. Cridge (known as 'Jerry') was born at Ross-on-Wye (his mother was visiting her parents at the time) in 1932. He spent his early years with his parents, Fred and Edna Cridge, brother Tony and sister Peggy at Aller Cottages, Tower Hill, Williton. His father served with the Royal Navy during the Second World War, and on his return was employed locally as a postman. Jerry attended St Peter's School, Williton, from 1937–47, and has penned the following article on his career and early days at Williton:

Whilst I attended St Peter's School some of the teachers were Mr W.J. White (headmaster), Mr R.V. Garland, Miss Tovey, Mrs E. Trebble, Miss Smith, Miss Huggins, Mrs Legge, Mrs Turner (née Boatright). I was a choirboy at St Peter's Church, helped pump the organ, rang the bells and was confirmed by the Bishop of Bath and Wells at Nettlecombe Church; Sunday School outings were a real treat.

The school gardens and poultry at Catwell were tended during school hours and also in the school holidays. I remember going out into the fields at Catwell and Stream to glean ears of corn left lying after threshing for the school poultry. This was done on a class basis by the elder girls and boys – good fun. Two prefab buildings were erected at the school which were used as extra classrooms, also one of them as a dining hall for school dinners.

John F. Cridge, 2004.

Whilst at school I had a spare time job delivering groceries for Mr A.J. Williams, whose shop was in High Street. This was accomplished by bicycle with a big basket in front, hence a small front wheel, which took some expertise to handle. Stogumber, Vellow, Sampford Brett, St Audries and Stream were some of the places requiring deliveries.

I remember the American Forces being at St Audries during the war years, and they laid on some parties with lots of goodies for the children.

Walnuts were always available at Christmas time from the trees at Eastfield House, chestnuts from the copse alongside the railway track near Torweston Farm, and mushrooms, in season, from the fields around Aller Cottages. We all helped during harvest time and I remember the cider, cheese, onions and new bread for the mid-day meal. Rabbits and pheasants were often caught when corn fields were cut.

Saturday afternoons were sometimes spent at the Conquest Cinema, Watchet – if we had the money! We walked from Williton to Watchet and it cost 6d (2.5p) to get in. I joined the ATC at Williton partly to get a uniform so that my age

was not questioned for adult films, and could take in my brother and sister. It worked sometimes! Watchet also boasted a Community Centre that held dances on Saturday evenings. Later in life, when on leave, I went to the Minehead Regal Ballroom, which had a sprung floor and a live band playing, and many a time a walk from Minehead to Williton had to be done due to missing the last bus! Weekly dance classes were run by the vicar at the Church Room, where I learnt old time dancing, amongst other things!

The old workhouse was then operating as a hospital for the aged (my mother worked there as an auxiliary nurse for 33 years). The Recreation Ground was a meeting place for all the boys and girls, especially at weekends. There were no houses north of Danesborough View, these being built in the late 1940s; Danesfield School was not even thought of, and part of the Methodist Church schoolroom was used as an overflow classroom.

After leaving school at Williton I began work at Staddon's Garage, Minehead, as a store boy for a short time before joining the Army Apprentices' College in 1948. I was posted to Norton Manor Camp, near Taunton, which had just been set up as a college for mainly 'A' trades. I was to be an architectural draughtsman, having passed the requisite education entrance for that type of trade. Whilst at the College (we moved to Harrogate after 18 months at Norton Manor) I gained all my 'O' and 'A' levels, which was to be of immense value later in my Army career. My main service from 1951 was with the Royal Engineers, spending some 33 years with the Corps before retiring prematurely as a major. I was also selected and served with the 'special forces' in the early years of my service, and thereafter in later years as required.

During my years with the Royal Engineers I qualified as a civil engineer and went on to get a MSc. in structural engineering. However, there came the time when I became disenchanted with Army life. I had remarried some five years earlier and had a young family; it was time to settle down permanently. After much soul searching and discussion with my wife we decided it was time to leave HM service as I could have served for another seven years. My wife had also been in the service as a Captain QARANC (Nursing Sister and Midwife) for 14 years. In 1978 we bought one of the ex-married officers' quarters at Liddymore and when we came home from Germany in April 1981 I registered as an engineer with the REDR (Register of Engineers for Disaster Relief). My first mission was to

Malaysia to build camps for the Vietnamese boat people under the auspices of the United Nations. The UN appreciated what I did for them, and took me on permanently as a consultant engineer, working in various countries of the world. This sort of work continued until 1998, so with my Army service of 33 years and then service with the UN of 19 years, I had a career span of *52 years, serving in many countries throughout the world.*

Jerry is now retired and, amongst other things, has devoted 20 years to the Royal British Legion. He lives with his wife at Cherry Tree Way, Watchet, and they have two daughters; he also has two daughters by a previous marriage.

Joe Strong was a former well-known Williton personality, always willing to give anyone a helping hand. After service with the Royal Navy escorting Baltic convoys during the Second World War, he was employed as a painter by local builders J. Chibbett & Sons. Joe became secretary of the Williton branch of the British Legion (later Royal) and was to the fore in helping organise the annual Whit-Monday gymkhana in aid of Legion funds.

Joe Strong, c.1950.

Interested in local government, he was for several years a member of the local Parish Council and one of the village's representatives on the old Williton Rural District Council, where he was a lively debater, always fighting hard for what he believed to be in the best interests of the village. Keen on soccer, he kept goal for Williton, and when his playing days were over he became a referee. Joe died at Bristol in 2003 in his 90s.

Edwin May was born at Henlade, near Taunton, in 1941, being the eighth child of 14. His family moved around West Somerset, with Edwin attending schools at Stogumber, Brompton Ralph, Wiveliscombe and finally at St Peter's, Williton, in 1952. Joining the 1013 Quantock Squadron ATC in 1954, Edwin is now a member of its civilian committee. He left school in 1956 and commenced work on a farm at Stogumber.

In 1959 he found employment at the Wansbrough Paper Mill at Watchet, where he gave over 40 years' split service, as he joined the County Ambulance Service for a while in the 1970s before returning to the mill. Whilst at the mill he volunteered for first aid duty, for which he received training at the Watchet Red Cross

Edwin May, 2006.

Centre. Edwin joined the Red Cross in 1968, still being a member at the time of writing. Two of the highlights of his time with the Red Cross were taking people who needed help on holiday and being asked to represent the local Red Cross at the Albert Hall Remembrance Service.

Edwin has represented Williton on the West Somerset District Council for two spells, and served in the cabinet for a while. He has also been a local parish councillor for several years, with periods as chairman. In 1963 Edwin married Brenda Peppin, of Williton, where they took up residence. They sadly lost their eldest daughter in 2005 after a long illness, but have two surviving daughters, also two grand-daughters and one grandson.

Fred Hutchings was chairman of West Somerset District Council in 1990–1991 and retired from it in 1999 after 25 years of service. He is pictured here holding the framed citation upon being made one of the first three honorary aldermen of the Council in 2002 in recognition of his 'eminent services to the council'. He had also served on its predecessor, Williton Rural District Council, since the 1960s and had been a member of Williton Parish Council for many years and a past chairman.

Born at Stogumber, Fred was educated at Huish's Grammar School, Taunton,

Fred Hutchings, 2002.

and was president of the Old Huish Association at the time of his death.

During the Second World War he served in Bomber Command of the RAF. Fred was a master butcher for almost 40 years, being a familiar face to many in his Williton Meat Supply shop.

A keen sportsman, he played cricket and football for Williton, Stogumber and Watchet and in later years played golf at Minehead. A keen marksman, he helped run local shoots until well into his 80s and won numerous trophies. Fred died at his Williton home in 2006, aged 89 years.

Left: *Head gardener David Langdon, of Williton, who tended the blooms in Minehead's award-winning Blenheim Gardens for more than 40 years, retired from his position in November 2004. David, known as 'Major', began his career in 1960 at the age of 16 with the former Minehead Urban District Council, transferring to West Somerset District Council following local government reorganisation in 1974, which found him taking on responsibility for the whole area.*

Walter Ashman of Half Acre, beside his home-grown monster spring cabbage in 1972. The cabbage weighed 15lbs with a circumference of 6ft 11ins (211 cms) and a diameter of 3ft 11ins (119cms). Walter had also grown 20-inch (51cms) long runner beans.

Watch out for the ogre up there, Annie! This giant sunflower, which reached a height of 14 feet, was grown by Philip and Annie Perry in 2004. Asked how he nurtured the plant, Philip replied: 'Frequent watering, with one part clean, one part dirty and one part my own!'

Three Williton Families

Above: *Langdon's Refreshment Tent, c.1910. Edwin ('Nobby') Boyles is second from left.*

Left: *Edwin ('Nobby') Boyles with bagpipes and unknown friend in the 1930s.*

Right: *Mr and Mrs Harry Burge and their son Jack. Harry was a well-liked and familiar Williton character and a keen follower of sport, particularly soccer, both locally and in higher spheres. For many years he was employed at the* West Somerset Free Press *works, where much leg-pulling and friendly banter would be exchanged, especially if Harry's beloved Bristol City had suffered defeat. Harry delivered thousands of newspapers around Williton in his time, including the much looked-forward-to Saturday evening sports papers, the* Pink 'Un *and* Green 'Un.

Henry John (Jack) Burge was born and bred at Williton. After leaving the local school he joined Williton solicitors Risdon's as a clerk, but then switched careers and joined the City of Bristol Police Force at the start of a remarkable career in which he travelled the world. During the Second World War Jack served as a captain in the Indian Army with the Frontier Force Rifles. It was then that he met his future wife Jane, who was with the Queen Alexandra Imperial Military Nursing Service, and they eventually went on to celebrate their golden wedding.

After the war, Jack rejoined the City of Bristol Police and in 1947 transferred to the Metropolitan Police. In 1953 he was appointed an inspector in the Colonial Police and served in Nyasaland (now Malawi) with the special branch. Two years later Jack and Jane moved to Cyprus with their young family (two sons and a daughter) and he was promoted to the rank of superintendent. Following his outstanding service there against the EOKA terrorists he

Jack Burge MBE

was awarded the MBE.

From Cyprus Jack was drafted into help oversee the break-up of the Federation of Rhodesia and Nyasaland in 1960. When it gained independence in 1963 he was asked to stay on and later was made an Assistant Commissioner with the Colonial Police and head of Interpol for East Africa. He retired from his distinguished service with the police in 1969 and moved back to West Somerset, becoming company secretary of Cox, Sons & Co. Ltd at Williton. Following the death of Mr Norman Cox, Jack was made general manager. He was closely involved in the negotiations for the company's takeover in 1979 by Sir Ray Tindle's group of family newspapers, its present owners, and retired in 1987.

Always very sport orientated, Jack was a keen footballer and cricketer with local clubs in his younger days. He was a founder-member of the Rotary Club of the Quantocks. Jack died in 1995, aged 73 years.

Watts family group at the Railway Hotel (now the Foresters Arms Hotel), 1902. Left to right, back row: Lilly, Fred, Daisy; middle row: Annie, May, Mrs Watts holding Henry, Mr J.O. Watts (landlord), James; front row: George, Sidney. All five sons served in the First World War, during which George died. Mr Watts received a letter from the King.

Born in Canada in 1926, Evelyn Watts is the third daughter of the late Mr James (Jim) Watts, formerly of Williton, and Mrs Watts; her grandfather, Mr J.O. Watts, was a former landlord of the Railway Hotel (now the Foresters Arms Hotel) at Williton. Evelyn's father emigrated to Canada at the age of 18, serving in the Royal NW Canadian Mounted Police; he joined the Canadian Forces during the First World War and served in France. After the war he married Harriet Maud Davis, of Yarde, and they both went to Canada. They had four children, all born in Edmonton, Alberta – Frances, Audrey, Edwin and Evelyn. Harriet died tragically in a fire in 1927 and the family returned to England, where the children were fostered by relatives. Mr Watts married Hilda Colwill in 1929 and she brought Evelyn up; her father died in 1937.

Evelyn resided in Half Acre and attended Williton School from 1931–37 where she passed a scholarship examination to Minehead County (later Grammar) School, which she attended from 1937–45. She then progressed to Westfield College, University of London, where she won an open exhibition. She obtained a BA Honours Degree in English in 1948 and a Teacher's Diploma in 1950. She has taught at Sandown Grammar School, Isle of Wight; Plymouth High School for Girls (head of English Department), while there she went on a teacher exchange to Los Cratos High School, California; Semiahmoo High School, White Rock, British Columbia, and King Edward VI Camp Hill School for Girls, Birmingham.

Recalling some of her growing-up days in Williton, Evelyn remembers Miss Smith, her infant teacher, and Mr W.J. White, the local headmaster, who coached her for the scholarship examination. He also took Betty Conibeer and herself to Dunster to sit the Ellsworth examination – they

Evelyn Watts, B.A.

came first and second! Mr White's children, June and Peter, used to call on her. Evelyn attended children's church on Sunday afternoons, supervised by the Revd Waggett, and recollects riding on Jones's baker's cart delivering bread with her Uncle Henry. Williton had a horse-drawn fire-engine at that time, and story has it that once when Watchet Fire Brigade came to help extinguish a fire, the Williton Brigade would not lend them any equipment with the consequence that the house burned down!

She also recalls weekend Girl Guide camps at Bridge Farm, meets of hounds at the Egremont Hotel, and children's Christmas parties at the Church Room with Mr Hensley (stationmaster) as Father Christmas. After a snowfall almost the whole village would go up to Pigeon Field for tobogganing – morning, afternoon and in the evening by moonlight. Also remembered are Tom Bellamy's jewellery and clockmaking shop at Bellamy's Corner and milk being delivered by Hibbert's from Watchet, the milk being dipped out of a churn into a jug. When a funeral cortege passed through the village everyone stood still and gentlemen removed their headgear as a mark of respect.

Evacuees arrived at the outbreak of the Second World War with Minehead County School having to take in Regent Street Polytechnic from London in the afternoons, resulting in Evelyn and her fellow pupils having only half a day's schooling for some years. Gas buses took them to Minehead, which were not much good on Somerset hills! The Guides helped in various ARP exercises and she remembers the Home Guard. One of her most poignant memories was D-Day – 6 June 1944. Evelyn is now retired and at the time of writing resides at Ryde on the Isle of Wight.

Church Life

Above: *St Peter's Church Choir, 1961.* Left to right: *Ralph White, Stella Locke, Sue Hurley, Kitty Clarke, Patsy Steer, Alison Chibbett, Pauline Pilcher, James Chibbett, Revd F.H. Hall.*

Right: *Mary Slade beside her magnificent floral display at St Peter's Church to celebrate the Queen's Golden Jubilee, 2002.*

Above: *St Peter's Church Choir, 1986.* The picture includes: *Brian Robertson, Revd John Andrews, Frank Morgan, Colin Chidgey, Jimmy Hurley, ? Arscott, Mrs Chibbett, Mary Slade and Harry Armstrong.*

Below: *Williton Methodist Sunday School Chirstmas party, 1939.*

Frank Morgan MBE was a churchwarden at St Peter's Church, Williton, for more than 30 years. Prior to that he was a churchwarden at Luxborough, before which he was vicar's warden at the naval base church at Scapa Flow. His 60 years' service to the Church was marked at St Peter's when he was presented with the Bishop's Shield, a rare honour. At the time of writing he is churchwarden emeritus. Frank has also been a recipient of the Royal Maundy Money and has given much service to the local community for which he was honoured with the MBE. In recognition of six decades of service to the Royal British Legion he was made a life member, the Legion's highest award, in 2007. Frank is also a life member of Quantock Rotary Club.

Frank Morgan (left) and Ralph White, 2002.

The late Ralph White was another stalwart of St Peter's, having served on the Parochial Church Council for many years, been a churchwarden, and a choir member for 60 years. A modest and much-loved man, Ralph farmed at Liddymore Farm, specialising in dairy cattle with a fine herd of Jerseys. His other interests included poultry and racing pigeons and he was secretary of the Watchet and Williton Pigeon Club. He later switched to show pigeons, breeding Dragoons.

Ralph was greatly involved with Dunster Show, spending many years on its committee. At the time of his death in 2006 he was researching the history of the Dunster Show Society, the show celebrating its 160th anniversary in that year. His widow Brenda has been a cattle steward at Dunster Show, and for 40 years or more Ralph was a steward at the Royal Bath and West Show. Very interested in local history, Ralph was an active member and past chairman of the West Somerset Village History Society and a member of the Watchet Market House Museum Society. He had also been a Special Constable for 22 years, a member of the Watchet and District Choral Society for 40 years and a juryman of Watchet Court Leet.

The opening in 2004 of Williton's first dedicated garden of rest next to St Peter's Church where ashes can be scattered or buried and where people can sit and remember their loved ones. Left to right: Beverley Machin (reader at St Peter's), Alan Chatfield and Sheelagh Spink (churchwardens), Revd Richard Allen (vicar), the Rt Revd Andrew Radford (Bishop of Taunton).

Williton Schools

Above: *St Peter's Junior School maypole dancing on the Recreation Ground in celebration of Queen Elizabeth's Coronation, 1953.*

Below: *Senior infants of St Peter's Junior School, 1963. Left to right, back row: ?, Nicholas Sully, Philip Wilkinson, ? Pilkington, David Cooke, Mrs Dennis, Norman Barnes, Christopher Sully, Kevin Smith, Stuart Barbour, Christopher Beaver, Stuart Chidgey; middle row: John Clarke, Clive Johnson, Mark Armstrong, Roger Massey, Brenda Foster, Claire Smith, Alison Slade, ?, Sheila Bellringer, Jayne Dickinson, Karen Beach, Andrew Thomas, Patrick Dennis, Frank Moores; front row: John Towells, Linda Treadwell, Mavis Kennington, Theresa Flewitt, Sylvia Williams, Barbara Foster, Lorna Hanniford, Beverley Beaver, Jane Ridler, ?, Sheila Coles, Susan Winter, Charles Takle.*

St Peter's Junior School, Class 4 (the senior class), 1965. Left to right, back row: David Brennan, Colin Barber, John Critchley, Ian White, Mr Hart (teacher), Robert Wheeler, David Bendon, John Chidgey, Chris Boyles; middle row: Pamela Newbert, Sylvia Parker, Penny Cheek, Georgina May, Christina May, Juliet Bendon, Deborah Toal, Catherine Doel, Rachel Hayes; seated on bench: Phyllis Arscott, Sonia Pugsley, Joy Tuckfield, Sandra Lewis, Maureen Stone, Heather Long, Marie Fitzpatrick, Alice Ansell, Susan Heywood; seated on ground: Ian Richards, Johnny Malik, Nigel ('Speedy') Wells, Martin Williams.

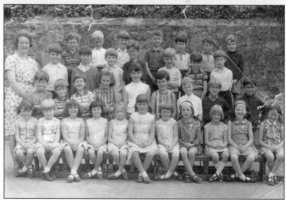

Above: *A class at St Peter's Junior School, 1966.*

Above: *Some pupils of St Peter's Junior School, 1967.*

St Peter's Junior School, c.1968. Left to right, back row: ?, ?, Dominic Hesp, Gary Eveleigh, Philip Lang, Stephen Masters, Gary Edbrook, ?, Patrick Richards; third row: Marcus Oakey, ?, Caroline Hole, Stephanie Lewis, Julie Haynes, Ann Williams, Gay Eveleigh, Jeremy Stone, Graham Wilcox; second row: Wendy Williams, Kim Watts, Zia Jane Smith, ?, Valerie Richards, Clair Prescott, Wendy McPerson, Susan Stephens; front row: Richard Palmer, Elvin Beaver, Kevin Grant, Paul Thomas, Dean Maddocks, Roger Boswell, Paul Sweetland.

Above: *St Peter's Junior School older pupils, 1969.*

Below: *St Peter's Junior School, younger pupils, 1969.*

Staff and pupils celebrated the tenth anniversary on 28 February 2006 of the official opening of St Peter's CE First School, Williton. Pictured with their grand anniversary cake, left to right: Verity Taylor, Thomas Hobbs, Val Ellis, James Peate (head), Alison Gould (cakemaker), George Sheldrake (past pupil).

Right: *Boys at Williton School gardens, Catwell, c.1928. Mr W.J. White (headmaster) is on the extreme right. Poultry were also kept at the gardens and had to be tended at holiday times as well as during term. Bungalows have since been built on this site.*

Left: *Section of the girls' PE display team at Williton School, 1949. Left to right, back row: Winnie Hill, Peggy Cridge, Joyce Stevens, Shirley Binding; middle row: Shirley Perkins, Maureen Tipper, Carol Willicombe, Irene Rowe, Doreen Darter, Miss P. Wheatley (teacher); front row: Iris Coombs, Janet Taylor, Joyce Webber, Valerie James.*

Right: *Williton Secondary Modern School rugby team, 1950. Left to right, back row: Chris Vine, Ken Moore, Terry Snell, A. Macauley, Roy Howells, Clive Smith, Edward Gibbs, Reg Lewis, Ken Shears, Edward Scott; front row: John Lillington, Chris Winter, Ken Grandfield, Robin Bex, Peter Burnett, Richard Labbe, Douglas Webber, Peter Simpson, Michael Routley.*

Senior pupils of Williton Secondary Modern School visit Bristol Zoo and Weston-super-Mare, 1950. Among those in the group are: Mr W.J. White (headmaster), Mr A.L. Kinsey, Mrs M. Coles, Mr H.G. Fry (teachers), K. Grandfield, W. Welch, D. Webber, R. Labbe, R. Lewis, R. Howells, B. Somerfield, R. Dennett, R. Bex, E. Gibbs, Elsie Fisher, Eleanor Jones, Pansy Langdon, Mary Newbert, Valerie James, Peggy Cridge, Sheila Reeder, Joyce Stevens, Iris Coombs, Margaret Pope, Marion Dyer.

Mr G.H. Fry's class at Williton Secondary Modern School, 1950. Left to right, back row: *K. Grandfield, W. Welch, P. Burnett, D. Webber, R. Labbe, C. Smith, E. Gibbs, R. Bex, R. Howells, A. Macauley, R. Lewis;* third row: *A. Coles, B. Somerfield, June Thomas, Pam Caley, Margaret Walford, Eleanor Jones, Iris Coombs, Edna Prescott, T. Snell, I Sully;* second row: *Elsie Fisher, Marion Dyer, Myrtle Mogford, Peggy Cridge, Valerie James, Joyce Stevens, Winnie Hill, Sheila Reeder, Doreen Coleman;* front row: *P. Simpson, C. Winter, C. Vine, A. Tregidgo, K. Shears, E. Nicholls, J. Lillington, M. Routley.*

Williton Secondary Modern School Soccer Players, 1956–57. Left to right, back row: *Mr G.H. Fry, George Corton, Duncan Morse, Kevin Convoy, Victor Hayes, Roger Lock, Adrian Burnell, Joseph Jenkins, Mr J.H. Thomas;* seated: *Colin Hill, Clive Tiller, William Calloway, Alan Yewer, Andrew Chilcott, William Chiplin, Thomas Bruford;* on ground: *Richard Bulpin, Michael Jones.*

Danesfield School Choir, 1979. Left to right, back row: *David Searle, Susan Shattock, Justine Grace, Kathleen Scott, Claire Butchers, ?, Wendy Mainwaring, Simon Webb;* middle row: *Hugh Crothers, Lucas Holloway, Joanne Chidgey, Lisa Patten, Annette Chidgey, Elizabeth Routley, Anita Rexworthy, Amanda Bennett, David Barrett, Adrian Filer;* front row: *Mandy Curtis, ?, Julia Day, Karen Knox, Jill Binding, Samantha Fouracre, Elizabeth Gill.*

Left: *A Danesfield School Tutor Group, 1983.* Left to right, back row: *Darren Williams, Edward Ridge, Mark Paul, Laurence Strong, ?, Robert Gould;* third row: *Matthew Mozeley, Andrew Jenkins, Lisa Chidgey, Ann McCutcheon, Joanne O'Sullivan, Samantha Milton, Perry Hobbs, Barry-John Davies;* second row: *Elisa Chave, Jennifer Stevens, Theresa Christian, Patricia Docherty, Samantha Searle, Naomi Elson, Eleanor Jones, Susan Wells;* front row: *Jason Perry, Simon Brewer, Stephen Tucker, Alex Nicholls, Simon Bale.*

Men At Work

Workmen digging a trench for the laying of sewerage pipes in Long Street, c.1920.

Above: *Some of Chibbett's building workers, c.1950s. Left to right: Alf Bulpin, Laurence Chorley, Percy Webber, Jack Chidgey, Cecil ('Sonny') Parsons, Ron Peppin, Wally Peppin, Dave Salter; front: ? (sub-contracted tiler).*

Left: *Williton workmen William Trebble (left) and Thomas Tipper at the excavation site at Battlegore (a field opposite Danesfield School) in 1931. Although extensive excavations were made, no direct evidence was found to link with the battle there against the Danes in AD918. Little else of any significance was found. The excavations were led by the distinguished Somerset archaeologist H. St George Gray, FSA, assisted by William Wedlake. Legend has it that the large stones at Battlegore were hurled there by a giant and the devil competing as to who could throw them the furthest from the Quantocks!*

West Somerset Free Press

Above: *Centenary dinner of the* West Somerset Free Press, *29 July, 1960. Among those at the top table (right) are Mr F.N. Cox (head of company and managing editor), Mr N.H.J. Cox (news editor) with Mrs Cox, and Mr H.A. Cox (director).*

Right: *Gathering of management and staff of the* West Somerset Free Press *at Halsway Manor, December 2004. Left to right, back row: Sara Mace, Annelise Yard, Gerry Baxter, Ann Tucker, Niki Wooldridge, John Lockyer, Dee Rickward, Ria Rickward, Cilla Webb, Mark Slack, George Donkin; middle row: Tony Knight, Gareth Purcell (editor), Reg Dickinson, David Tucker, Sir Ray Tindle (head of Farnham Castle Newspaper Group), Brian Doel, David Knell, Catherine Boukfil, Marie Downing, Keith Towells; front row: Nick Sully, Moira Jones, Zari Evans, Sue Barnes, David Sully.*

Above: *E.W. (Ted) Stevens being presented with retirement gifts from* West Somerset Free Press *colleagues by Bill Groves (foreman) in 1966. Ted had completed 50 years' service at the* Free Press *printing works. He was also given a gift of his choice by the then proprietors, Cox, Sons & Co Ltd. Left to right: Maurice Chidgey, Arthur Sully, Ken Grandfield, Keith Towells, Ted Stevens, Bill Groves, Alf Bulpin.*

Group pictured in 1980 after a lunch and presentation to Jack Hurley to mark his retirement and 50 years of service to the West Somerset Free Press. *He began there as a junior reporter in 1930 and rose to become editor. It was Jack who brought to life the remarkable character of Will Widden, who appeared at the foot of his weekly 'Notes by the Way' column. Jack was awarded the MBE for services to local journalism. Left to right, back row: ?, Jeff Cox, Arthur Sully, Jack Burge MBE, Bob Alwyn (news editor), George Hale, ?, Maurice Chidgey, Dennis Stone; front row: Mrs Pat Cox, Sir Ray Tindle (head of the Tindle Newspaper Group), Jack Hurley, Reg Dickinson, Mrs Dickinson.*

One of the last printer's apprentice 'banging out ceremony' (when an apprenticeship was completed) at the West Somerset Free Press *works, Williton, 1979. Left to right, back: Roy Chave, Nigel Ridler, 'victim' David Milton, Richard McNally, Michael Selley; kneeling: David Sully and David Parkman.*

Working for the Community

Former sub-postmaster Edgar Farmer, c.1950.

Former sub-postmaster Norman Lovett, c.1965.

Former sub-postmaster Frank Morgan, MBE.

Above: Telephone exchange girls at Williton Post Office, 1945. Left to right: Barbara Hayes, Margery Farmer (daughter of sub-postmaster Edgar Farmer), Joan Chorley, Vera Morse.

Left: Mr and Mrs Edgar Farmer and daughter Margery in their garden behind Williton Post Office, c.1935. Mr Farmer was sub-postmaster at Williton for many years.

Former Parachute Regiment platoon sargeant Bert Pearson, of Williton, was rewarded in 2007 for decades of service to the community. He received the Lord Lieutenant's Award for services to the cause of ex-Servicemen and women and their dependents.

PC Norman Ackland, of Williton, standing beside a police patrol car, 1969.

Williton Fire Brigade after attending the great blaze at Wansbrough Paper Mill, Watchet, in 1898.

Police Sergeant Frederick Charles Woolley, who was stationed at Williton in the 1920s and 1930s and retired there.

Right: *Williton Fire Brigade, c.1963. Driver: Philip Perry; looking out of engine: Frank Hawkins; left to right, back row: Station Officer W. Symonds, V. Buller, R. Binding, R. Melhuish, K. Buller, A. Williams, C. Trebble, P. Brewer, J. Bryant, B. Trebble; front row: D. Sully, K. Bulpin, D. Howells, J. Smith, J. Tickner, D. Chidgey, C. Tarr.*

Left: *Members of Williton Red Cross pictured outside Halsway Manor, c.1950. Among those pictured are: Mrs W. Cotterell, Miss K. Ward, Mrs G. Allen, Mrs D. Prole, Miss W. Binding, Miss M. Hurley, Mrs. E. Smith, Mrs W. Sparkes, Mrs Stoate.*

Right: *Some members and guests attending the last meeting of Williton Court Leet at the New Inn (now the Royal Huntsman) in 1953. Anti-clockwise: L.A. Lang, Lewis Bale, Fred Gibbons, W.H. Ashman, Dr C.F.R. Killick, N.H.J. Cox, ?, Revd Frank H. Hall, H.J. Coles, G.C. Wyndham (lord of the manor), Percy Hutchings, Tom Warren, J.E. Hurley, Wilfred Warren, Gordon Hutchings, Cyril Richards.*

Left: *Past chairmen of Williton Rural District Council from 1944–74 seen at the council's last civic dinner before the formation in April 1974 of West Somerset District Council. Left to right: Major T.F. Trollope-Bellew, Mrs D.M. Clarke, Mr H.M. Thomas, Mr H.J. Chibbett (last chairman), Mr J.W. Rawle, Mr J.J. Hayman, Mr J.K. Kidler, Mr F.P. Risdon (former clerk), Mr J.M. Sansom (clerk).*

Williton At War

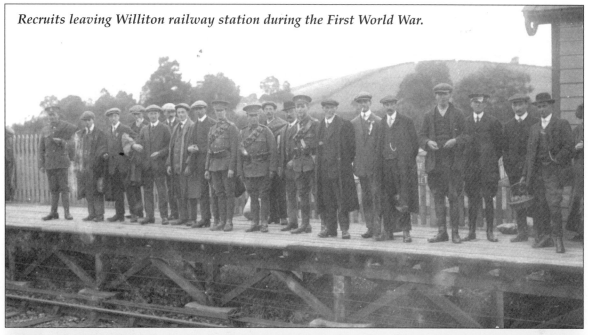

Recruits leaving Williton railway station during the First World War.

Above: *Officers and staff of No. 4 (Williton) Company Home Guard, 1944. Left to right, back row: Ernest Stevens, ?, Sgt Major Bill Venn, Mrs Beryl Venn, Cyril Thomas, Margaret Branchflower, Maude Trebble, Bill Thomson, ?, Stan Baker; front row: Sidney Connett, Jack H. Bissell, Victor Danby, Bill Hurley, Major W.T. Greswell, Col E.R. Clayton, CMG, DSO, Dr J. Erskine Collins (medical officer), Edwin Herbert Davis.*

Right: *Officers of Williton Girls' Training Corps in the early 1940s. Left to right, back: Barbara Chapman, Marguerite Edwards, Doreen Conibeer, June White; front row: Hilda Griffiths, Mrs A. Lovelace, Mary Bale.*

Distribution of ration books by ambulance from Williton Council Offices, 1943. Left to right: Jack Binding, Alice Jukes, ?, Dorothy Pullin, Sylvia Carpenter, Josephine Knipe, W. Chalice (ambulance driver).

Right: *Unveiling ceremony of the plaque on a wall of the war memorial shelter on the Recreation Ground to honour Williton Servicemen who fell during the Second World War, c.1950s. Left to right: Dr C.F.R. Killick, G.C. Wyndham, Revd F.H. Hall, Revd D. Gourley Thomas, H.J. Chibbett, E.G. Conibeer.*

Left: *In June 2007 Williton's first memorial monument was unveiled by the village's Royal British Legion president Frank Morgan. The Celtic cross-topped Edinburgh granite structure is in honour of the 36 men of the Williton area who died during two world wars and their names are featured on it. More than 100 people gathered at the Recreation Ground for the long-awaited ceremony. A service of dedication was led by the vicar of Williton, the Revd Richard Allen, supported by the Methodist minister, the Revd Gareth Davies, and the Roman Catholic deacon, the Revd Vincent Woods. The monument is sited in front of the war memorial shelter that was dedicated 75 years earlier. Poppy wreaths were laid by Cllr Derek Cridland on behalf of Williton Parish Council, Cllr Jenny Hill, chairman of West Somerset Council, and Bert Pearson, chairman of Williton RBL. Children from Danesfield Middle and St Peter's CE First Schools were among those who laid tiny crosses around the memorial at the end of the ceremony. Left to right, back row: Katherine Peeks and Eliza Bryant (Danesfield School), Henry Stone (standard bearer), Frank Morgan, Mike Wool (deputy Somerset standard bearer), Bert Pearson; kneeling: Ella Curtis and Chris Kelly (St Peter's CE First School).*

The British Legion and Women's Institute

Frank Morgan, Royal British Legion Williton branch chairman, presents a cake to Women's Section chairman Mary Stockham to mark its 75th anniversary in 2002. The Women's Section was also presented with a certificate to mark 75 years of existence in Williton. Left to right, back row: *Audrey Scrace, Jean Farnes, Isobel Haynes, Muriel Seabrook, Pam Stephens, Connie Paige, Gina Bruford, Edith Parsons, Flossie Hall, Emily Hawkins, Phyllis Towells, Margaret Leavy;* front row: *Kath Edwards, Mary Fisher, Amelia Langdon, Betty May.*

Williton British Legion Rifle Club, late 1950s. Left to right, back row: *Fred Hutchings, David Biggs, Bill Pugsley;* front row: *Cyril Metson, John Atton, Maurice Bryne.*

Above: *Williton Women's Institute Party, c.1965.* Left to right: *Gladys Pullin, Gertie Coles, ?, May Ashman, Sue Lee, Lilian Braunton, Betty Armstrong, Iris Peppin, Joan Baker.*

Above: *Williton Women's Institute banner, presented by Miss Rogers in 1937 to commemorate the Coronation of King George VI. It was carried on Coronation Day by Mrs Western, with Mrs Chapman and Mrs Tiller as assistants.*

Right: *A group of Williton Women's Institute members visiting Broadway Village Hall on Denman College Day in 2004.* Left to right: *Muriel Stone, Pearl Morrison, Jean Barbour, Angela Cook, Ann Smith, Jenny Handisyde, Pam Farmer, Jean Hill, Valerie Broomfield.*

Celebrations and Get-Togethers

Tableau at Williton in celebration of King George V's Silver Jubilee, 1935. Left to right, back row: *Miss Sawyer, Frances Buckingham, Mabel James, Mrs Langdon, ?, Muriel Date, Mildred Welsher, Dorothy Welsher, Joan Langdon, Peggy Beare, Miss M. Bushen, Mrs Salter;* middle row: *Blanche Salter, Miss Best, Phyllis Bolt, Mrs Hayes, Miss Maslin, Florrie Gardner, May Buckingham;* front row: *Beryl Luck, ?, Mary Richards, Peggy Hughes, Yvonne Bourne, Mary Bale, Barbara Hayes, Joan Chorley, Barbara Chapman, Sylvia Richards, Betty Conibeer, Peggy Stone.*

Above: *Coronation Day parade, 1937.*

Right: *Some Williton residents celebrating the Coronation of Queen Elizabeth II with a supper in the Church Room, 1953.* Front left are: *Mrs Vi Jones and Mrs Joe Strong.*

Above: *Queen Elizabeth's Silver Jubilee celebrations at Williton, 1977.*

Above: *Fancy dress entrants at the Recreation Ground in celebration of the Queen's Silver Jubilee, 1977.* Left to right: *Dawn (just visible) and Gail Beaver, Helen Short, Ken Stephens, Jeanette Whittington, Alison Mayer, Elizabeth Newton.*

Left: *Geraldine (left) and Tracey Williams with their first prize-winning decorated bicycle at the Williton Queen's Silver Jubilee celebrations, 1977.*

Competitors for Williton's Festival Queen in connection with the village's celebrations for Queen Elizabeth II's Silver Jubilee, 1977. Left to right: *Linda Guyton, Christine Cridland, Donna Guyton, Anne Coles, Valerie Jones, Betty Sheehan, Dina Hall, Linzi Mayer, Linda Arscott, Esta Hunt, Angela Richards, Janice Garrard, another Angela Richards, Gillian Jones, Jill Catney;* seated: *Festival Queen Sue Hammond.*

Above: *Some of the residents of Danesborough View celebrating the Queen's Golden Jubilee in the Community Room, 2002.*

Above: *Climbing high during the Queen's Golden Jubilee celebrations in Williton, 2002. Left to right: Jemma Fitzgerald, Kirsty Potter, Rupert Bailey, Chloe Knight, Rebecca Nicholls.*

Above: *Part of the crowd on the Recreation Ground celebrating the Queen's Golden Jubilee, 2002. In the centre foreground are: Sandra Coombs and Janet Beaver.*

Above: *Christmas party at the Church Room in the 1950s, with Edgar Farmer in the front.*

Left: *Christmas celebrations at Croft House, Williton, c.1975. Left to right, standing: Brenda Veysey, Marion Gibbs, Bill Grove, Shirley Williams, Elsie Calloway, 'Dinney' Moore, Carol Parsons, Ernie Hayes, Joan Pugsley, Maisie Johnson, Emily Stark, Daphne Johnson, Jean Harris, Eileen Cridland, Margaret Wilkinson.*

Below: *An early children's charabanc outing. Sat behind the driver is Ted Ashman.*

Brownies, Guides and Scouts

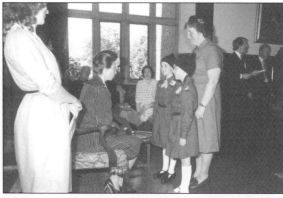

Williton Brownies presenting a bird nesting box to Croft House, 1973. Left to right, back row: *Shirley Williams, Betty Coggins, Bill Grove (superintendent), Jane Grove;* front row: *Kay Shepstone, Geraldine Williams, Nicola Shepstone, Brenda Richards, Tracey Williams, Sarah Mason.*

Princess Anne at Dunster Castle receiving Williton Brownies' purse containing £50 as their contribution to Save the Children Fund, 1985. The Brownies are Allergo Monaco and Sarah Bruford watched by Leader Shirley Williams.

Right: *Geraldine Williams (left) and Virginia Yandle at the Guide/Brownie Gang Show at Danesfield School, late 1970s.*

1st Williton Guides and 2nd Williton Brownies at the Guide/Brownie Gang Show at Danesfield School, mid-1970s. Left to right, back row: *Alison Coombs, Kay and Nicola Shepstone, Karen Tiller, Rosilyn May, Linda Harris, Lynda Leach, Debbie May, Karen Lewis, Geraldine Williams, Carrie Slater;* front row: *Wendy Quince, Kim Bradbury, Penny Ford, Lisa Vassiliou, Tracey Saunders, Joanne Mossman, Jane Bishop, Santina Docherty, Mandy Lang, Tracey Burnett, Paula Hayes.*

Left: *1st Williton Girl Guide Company, 1939.* Left to right, back row: *Mollie Hurley, Barbara Chapman, Maureen Bevan, Rita Chidgey;* third row: *Betty Tarr, Sylvia Pullin, Amy Webber, Marjorie Cook, Evelyn Watts, Sylvia Wakefield, Barbara Luck, Betty Conibeer, Dorothy Burnell, Dorothy Sully, Kathy Brown, Mary Langdon;* second row: *Peggy Hughes, Joan Holborough, Yvonne Bourne, Barbara Hayes, Miss Kathleen Ward, Miss Spry, Betty Yeandle, Vera Morse, Peggy Stone, Mary Bale;* front row: *Betty Holborough, Joan Chorley, Gladys Webber, Mary Ashman, Jean Stevens, Mary Davis, Joan Greenslade, Beryl Luck, Edna Clark, Sylvia Buckingham.*

Williton Girl Guides, the guests of Watchet Sea Scouts, c. 1956. Left to right, back row: *?, Stella Locke, Anne Alderson;* middle row: *Diane Nethercott, Patsy Steer, Ann Maxfield;* front row: *Sue Hurley, Diane Orr, ?, Daphne Alderson, Sally Cattle.*

Williton Girl Guides, 1958. Left to right: *Ann Trebble, ?, Jane Hutchings, Sheila Tipper, ?, Sue Hurley, ?, Margaret Chibbett, Sally Cattle, Daphne Alderson, Alison Chibbett, Liz Reynolds, Pauline Pilcher, Cynthia Reynolds, Sue Fry, Mary Stockham.*

Williton Girl Guides reunion, c.1960. Left to right, back row: *Kathleen Ward, Marjorie Pearse, Gertie Coles, May Ashman, Gwen Pullin, Mrs Sparks, ?, ?, ?, Margaret Wheeler;* middle row: *Margaret Hurley, Ethel Watts, ?, ?, Gladys Bellamy, Gertie Allen, Blanche Salter;* front row: *Margie Bryne, ?, Ethel Branchflower, ?.*

Geraldine Williams cutting the cake in honour of her becoming a Queen's Guide, c.1983. Left to right, back row: *Hazel Pink, Betty Smythers, Geraldine Williams, Shirley Williams, Wendy McPherson, Joyce Martin, Margaret Shepstone, Janet Beaver, Debbie May;* front row: *Nicola Shepstone, Mandy Dochery, Toria Phillips, Rachel Evans, Jane Watts, Jane Bishop, Sharon Phillips, ?.*

Above: *Williton Scouts, c.1940s. Left to right: Maurice Chidgey, Raymond Hunt, Michael Chapman, Ken Grandfield, John Burnett (Scoutmaster), John Scott, Tony Cridge.*

Above: *The 1st Williton Scout Patrol Archilleans, winners of the 1998 Somerset Jamboree County Flag and the West Somerset District Shield. Left to right, back row: Aaron Brooksbank, Noel Mullally, Patrol Leader Tom Rivett, Oliver Kerslake; front row: Richard Tennant, Jerome Rosling.*

Right: *Williton Scout Martin Patterson, who attended the World Scout Jamboree in Chile in 1999 (pictured centre), with the Williton Beaver Colony on his return in January 2000. Left to right, back row: Laurence Chidley, Andrew Martin, Nicholas Hill, Rachael Ince, Ben Parsons, Moss Tilley, Michael Hutchinson, Rupert Bailey, Stephen Nesbitt-Price, Sean O'Sullivan, William Tennant; middle row: Andrew Covey, Grant Ridler, Martin Patterson, Emily Sheldrake, Andew Miles; front row: William Cooke, Matthew Langbein, Thomas Salvidge, Robert Lockyer, Rebecca Tennant, Sydney Morse, ?.*

Above: *Williton Scouts and Cubs before they set off on the Quantocks link activity in 1986. Left to right, back row: Sheila Clavey, Mark Rush, Darren Williams, Mark Duddridge, Richard Rigden, Philip Rigden, Nick Lewis, ?, Jonathan Plumbley, Paul Rush, Royston Craig, David Scott, Sue Upstone, Mary Duddridge; middle row: Simon Upstone, Philip Blake, Simon Dennis, Simon Machin, Nicky Gould, Brendon Docherty; front row: Stephen Bellamy, Christopher Bellamy, Adam Duddridge, Carl Chilcott, Charles Sincock, Steven Duck, Luke Duddridge.*

Above: *Venture and Beaver Scouts after being presented with awards by District Commissioner Martin Harborne during the 1998 Williton Scout Group annual carol service. Karen Hayes and Vanessa Bowden made history in West Somerset scouting as they are the first girls to join a local scout group. Left to right, back row: Scout Leader Steve King, Venture Scout Victoria Sunderland, District Commissioner Martin Harborne, Venture Scout Leader Graham Bunting; middle row: Venture Scouts Luke Duddridge, Michael King, Vanessa Bowden, Karen Hayes; front row: Beaver Scouts Sean O'Sullivan, Moss Tilley, Rachael Ince, Michael Hutchinson.*

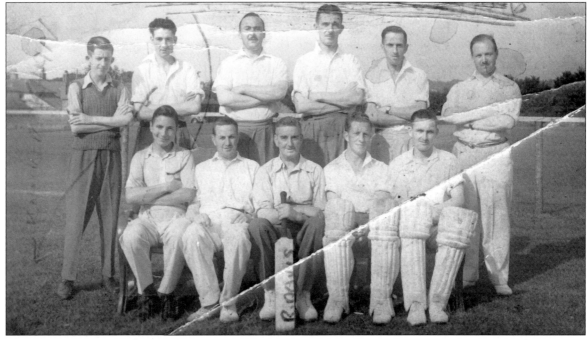

West Somerset Free Press *Cricket Team, 1947.* Left to right, back row: *Raymond Hunt, Bill McCord, Jack Hurley, Bob Parsons, Arthur Sully, Norman Cox;* front row: *Gordon Allen, Cyril Woolley, Reg Davis, Bill Groves, Chris Sansom.*

Williton Cricket 1st XI, 1956. Left to right: *Bill McCord, Jim Steer, John Thomas, Peter Armstrong, Ray Braunton, Ken Grandfield, Maurice Chidgey, Haydn Sully (later Somerset and Northants), Robin Wood, George Webber, Harry Bowles;* front row: *David Sansom (scorer).*

Williton cricketers, winners of the Porlock Six-a-Side Competition, 1960. Left to right, back row: *David Sully, Ray Braunton, Ken Grandfield, John Holroyd;* front row: *Laurie Wilson, Harry Bowles, David Beach.*

Left: *Williton cricket team, 1964.* Left to right, back row: *Robert Hutchings, Ken Grandfield, Laurie Wilson, ?, Maurice Chidgey, Edward Down;* seated: *Jack Sansom, Ray Braunton, Chris Sansom, David Sully;* on ground: *Anthony Maddocks.*

Sport and Leisure

Cricket

Above: West Somerset Free Press *cricket team in the 1970s.* Left to right: *Jack McTiffin, Alan Burge, Chris Sansom, Michael Hayes, Clayton Williams, Ian Burge, Roy Chave, Maurice Chidgey, Steve Kirby, Jack Burge, Vic Pollard (New Zealand Test player).*

Right: *The Revd Richard Allen, Williton's cricket-loving vicar. In his playing days Richard was a lively fast bowler, his last club being Minehead. At the time of writing he umpires in the West of England Premier and West Somerset Cricket Leagues.*

Below: *Williton Cricket Team, 1981.* Left to right, back row: *Alec Danby, Robin Illingworth, Dean Maddocks, Roger Green, Rod Richards, Mike Rawle;* front row: *Phil Watts, Colin Richards, Chris Polsom, Nick Nation, John Byrne.*

Football

Gliddon's and Parsons & Hann's Football Team on the Recreation Ground, c.1937, probably playing a team from the West Somerset Free Press. *Left to right, back row: ?, H. Hann, H. Isaac, M. Tiller, F. Baker, J. Gliddon, E.J. Bale (referee); front row: V. Hislop, M. Boyles, C.T. Hann, ?.*

Williton Football team, c.1937–38. Left to right, back row: ?, W.C. Hurley, G. Tipper, ?, R.C. Parsons, W. Sully, H.W. Phare, ?, T. Rawle (referee); middle row: G. Sweet, A. Caley, W. Tipper, C.W. Doble, W. Groves; front row: W. Gardner, F. Doble.

Williton Youth football team, mid-1950s. Left to right, back row: Redvers Besley (manager), Colin Hill, ?, John Branchflower, J. Bull, Peter Williams; middle row: ?, David Sully; front row: Trevor Nethercott, ?, Tony Paull, Colin Richards, John Jenkins.

Williton Football Team, Taunton and District League winners, 1966. Left to right, back row: John Warburton, John Branchflower, Peter Williams, David Sully, Peter Armstrong, Richard Sherrin, Alan Bellamy (secretary), Colin Norman; front row: Robin Strong, John Holroyd, Trevor Nethercott, Tom Bruford, Billy Calloway.

John Holroyd (back left) presenting Peter Armstrong with a pen and pencil set at Williton Football Club's dinner in 1967 to mark his retirement from the Club, for which he had played 700 matches. Seated left: Mr George Wyndham (president) and an official from Taunton and District Saturday League with his wife.

Some of the diners at Williton Football Club dinner at the Egremont Hotel, 1967. Among those pictured are: Peter and Betty Armstrong, Alan Bellamy, Irene Thorne, Trevor Nethercott, Richard Sherrin, Sheila Chubb, David Sully, Robert Yandle, Mrs Isaac, David Taylor.

1013 Quantock Squadron ATC Football Team, 1949. Left to right, back row: Norman Jones, ?, Danny Bryan, Eric Binding, Stan Balch, Brian Redd, David Reed, Tony Horsey, Geoff Griffin, Ken Bowden, Bill Court; front row: Bill Mattravers, Trevor Beaver, Alec Danby, Billy Sherlock, Norman Binding, Donald Webber, Terry Peppin, Mervyn Parsons.

Edward Martin's first Football League appointment as an assistant referee, Plymouth Argyle v York City, 1996. Left to right: Edward Martin, Rob Harris (referee), Lee Baker.

Edward Martin, well-known Williton business-man and resident, decided to go into soccer refereeing entirely by accident. He had always enjoyed playing football, but admits he was never that good at the game. The highlight of his playing career was keeping goal for Somerset College of Arts and Technology for the term he was there. After a break from playing for several years, he signed up to play for the newly-formed Foresters Arms team at Williton, which entered the Taunton Sunday League. He struggled to make the starting 11 and usually ended up as a substitute. The opposition usually turned up with just 11 players and if no referee was available it was left to him to officiate or there would have been no match for the other 22. After a few games as a makeshift referee and with some encouragement from local referee Mervyn Parsons, he enrolled on a referees' course in Bridgwater and, after completing the course, started refereeing in the Taunton Saturday League.

Edward progressed into the Somerset Senior League and the Western League and was in a team with other West Somerset officials, Lee Baker, Martin Strong, Andrew Escott and Mike Kelly. He was appointed onto the Football League list of assistant referees at the end of the 1995 season, his first game being Plymouth Argyle v York City in Division Two in August, 1996. The moment was very special as the other assistant referee was another local lad, Lee Baker.

Edward was lucky enough to officiate in many high profile games, including several that were shown on live television and he met many stars of the game. All games were extremely high-pressured and he was involved in many ups and downs, being attacked and knocked unconscious by a spectator in the match between Portsmouth and Sheffield United after advising the referee to send off the Sheffield United goalkeeper. He has been involved in many local derby matches, including Bristol City v Bristol Rovers, Exeter City v Torquay United, Cardiff City v Swansea City, Bristol City v Swindon Town. Edward has refereed in the Conference South Division and in a match between Basingstoke and Weymouth all was quiet until the last five minutes when he had to send off a goalkeeper, caution his replacement, award a penalty and deal with a crowd invasion.

The most bizarre game Edward refereed involved Williton and Bridgwater Dukes – it lasted just 22 minutes! He sent off one of the Dukes' players and then all the Dukes walked off and refused to play. Edward is often asked which was the most important game that he officiated in. He believes there were many, but on the last day of the 2003 season either Swansea City or Exeter City, depending on the results, would be relegated from the Football League to the Conference. He was appointed to the game between Swansea City v Hull City, the ground was full to capacity and the atmosphere electric. From his perspective the game went well and Swansea won. The match assessor was Jim Ashworth, his boss at the Football League, and he summed up his match report with the comment, 'That on this performance I have no advice to offer.'

Unfortunately, recurring calf muscle injuries ended his refereeing career at the end of the 2005 season after serving for 10 years on the Football League circuit. Edward, like his father before him, has also played cricket for Watchet for many years.

Other Sports and Pastimes

The Colts, members of Williton Club Skittles' League, cup winners 1957. Left to right, back row: George May, Jack Warre, Ken Oakey, Gordon Hall; front row: Bob Trebble, Joe Court, Bill Court, Harry Isaac, Arthur ('Bungy') May.

Press Boys Skittles Team, 1978. Left to right, back row: Roger Willis, David Sully, Mark Slack, Roy Chave; front row: Keith Towells, Nigel Ridler, Maurice Newbert.

Williton Club, winners of the Watchet and District Skittles League Division A (now Premier), 1979–80. Left to right, back row: David Sully, Roger Willis, Brian Bellamy, Chris Auton; front row: Nigel Bray, Keith Bulpin, David ('Major') Langdon.

Wranglers Skittles team, runners-up Watchet and District Skittles League, Premier Division, 1999–2000. Left to right, back row: D. Sully, G. Sloman, A. Bland, C. Towells; front row: G. Perkins, B. Arthington, A. Bulpin, N. Sully.

Right: Mitchell Clarke (left) and Paul Dennis after completing the New Forest Marathon alongside 556 other runners in 2002.

Below: High jinks in the wheelbarrow race at St Peter's Church Fête, 1957. Schoolteacher L.A. Lang is on the far left.

Sports at Williton Church Fête, 1951.

Albert Edward Bulpin with his milk-cart which won first prize at Williton Gymkhana in 1929. On one side is painted 'A.E. Bulpin, Milk Retailer, Sampford Brett Dairy'.

Cyril Bulpin showing a grey Shire horse at Williton Gymkhana in 1950.

Various people attending a black Shire horse at Williton Gymkhana in the 1950s. Left to right: Dickie Davis, Cyril Bulpin, Leonard Chidgey, Bill Coles.

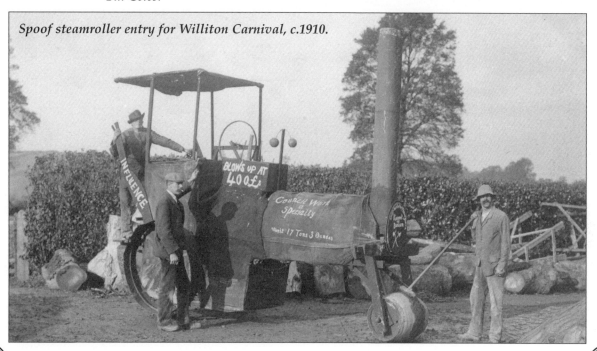

Spoof steamroller entry for Williton Carnival, c.1910.

145

Williton Drum and Fife Band in the early part of the last century.

GFS Folk Dance Team, 1946. Left to right, back row: Evelyn Watts, Margaret Burnell, Marjorie Cook, Betty Braunton; front row: Sylvia Burnett, Pam Besley, Mrs M. Mason, Pam Kerslake, Daphne Pullin.

Williton Majorettes, c.1990. The Majorettes were formed in 1984 by teenagers Michelle (back, far left) and Tracey Saunders (back, second from right), but were disbanded in 1996. They trained at Danesfield School and took part in local carnivals, fêtes, parades and competitions with their baton-twirling, marching and pom-pom routines.

Tableau representing Sir Francis Drake returning to claim his bride, Elizabeth Sydenham, from a local suiter at Williton's celebration of the Festival of Britain, 1951. Left to right: Harry Armstrong, Doreen Conibeer, Deric Gibbons.

Cast of the musical comedy Transatlantica, *written and produced by Williton schoolteachers David Beach (lyrics) and John Holroyd (music), which was presented by Williton Players to packed houses at the local Secondary Modern (now Danesfield) School in 1963. Those pictured are: Harry Armstrong, Molly Hudson, Gordon Frankland, Jennifer Evans, Susan Lee, David Beach, Laurie Wilson, Roland Garside, Chris Collier, Dennis Whitely, Peter Witts, Julia Polsom, John Morgan, Jimmy Hurley, Kay Pearce, Judy Young, Terry James, Jeanne Donnan, Sonia Armstrong, Sue Hurley, Jenny Tipper, Pat Steer, Lee Ackland, Hilary McNeil, Valerie Heggs.*

Chapter 4

THE OUTSKIRTS

Doniford

The following article appeared in the *West Somerset Free Press* in 1965. It was written by Jack Hurley, later to become editor of the paper:

Doniford beach – where Williton meets the sea! The slipway in this 1920s photograph has long been washed away and the donkey house has disappeared.

There is always danger in the sweeping generalisation. We are told that people demand sophisticated pleasures these days, but if that were wholly true the mums and dads of Williton would not be taking to the Doniford road in such numbers each summer. Their rendezvous – a little beach where their forebears found pleasure. We could say, with an air, 'St Donat's Ford', but Doniford will do! If one thinks of beach joys in terms of surrounding chalet camps, then Williton's little watering-place is the poor relation between Helwell Bay and St Audries Bay, yet Doniford's popularity with the local population on a summer's afternoon or evening would come as a surprise to any who had not ventured there for years. The beach is not endowed with nothing that nature herself did not put there; one may not buy candy-floss, whelks, hot-dogs or jugged tea from a beach stall, take a boat on a marine lake, or put the kids on the back of a donkey. Instead, the children take what Doniford offers in its natural state – and are perfectly satisfied with the basic elements. The parents find it the cheapest of all day trips, and one of the most relaxing.

The water is the good old channel grey, but colour perception is probably not highly developed in a child; it is sufficient that water is water anywhere! The swimming is good and safe, and when the tide seems to have retreated insociably far the children wait contentedly for its return, lost in the splashy delights of rock pools, in the thrills of turning up the little crabs that only pretend to bite. And, if you have never seen an expanse of golden sand, you will not miss its absence at Doniford. You can sift the shingle. Lest this sounds like a 'commercial', one should hasten to add that it is merely a thought upon the simplicity of a day upon an unpretentious beach that seems to have taken on a fresh lease of life as part of Williton's recreation amentities; and also a memory of the scene and days enjoyed by our ancestors.

Some of us knew the Doniford slipway in the picture – that incline up which the donkeys were led with their panniers bearing limestones. The slipway was mercilessly buffeted and battered away in the early 1920s when perhaps it might have been saved by a stitch in time. (Note the place where the wall began to give.) Yes, we knew the old Doniford road, or lane, starting at the Mason's Arms with a bad smell on a hot day from a cess drain covered only by a trap-door. A rough and stony road, belonging to the lazy carthorse and the sleepy carter, before the Army transport of the 1920s and 1930s placed the meandering walker in peril. We sauntered, whole families of us, down that winding Doniford road, under the railway bridge where fingers of cement still hang like little stalactites; past the stream wall on the left in which is set a indecipherable inscription in stone; past the 'weeping tree' at the farm, and to the first whiff of seaside and seaweed. Doniford was the Williton child's first seaside. Or perhaps, for a change, we followed the Swill River along by Egrove Farm, where the sand martins made their holes in the banks, and the occasional kingfisher dazzled the eye in a blue, explosive flash.

And here was Doniford, Romano-British settlement in the time of Constantine, and, much later, a manor granted by Richard Fitzurse to William de Regni, of Aisholt. Doniford, where Pulman had his cloth factory, many millions of years after the Ichthyosaurus deposited its fossil! Doniford, where 100,000 [of] years ago the great hairy elephants roamed, and where one of them left a tooth a foot long to be found in the 19th century by a Williton workhouse inmate. The fearsome mammoths gave way in another era to the gentle donkey, beast of burden in the lime-burning that flourished all along this coast. The donkey house on the cliff top above the old slipway can be seen in the picture; close by were the lime-kilns, cold and silent now, crumbling grey battlements by the side of the approach track to the cliff edge.

The Free Press tells of Doniford's popularity in the 19th century for beach parties, picnics, and boating. A century ago the St Decuman's Lodge of Oddfellows held their annual fete at Doniford – and went by train from Williton. Where the train set the people down is not known, and the railway company never made Doniford an official halt as a result. Fifty years ago this week the Williton Wesleyan Circuit picnic had Doniford as the venue – with tea in the hay-carpeted waggon shed of Doniford Farm. St Peter's Church Sunday School held annual treats on the shore, and in the field between the farm and the Swill banks the Watchet Baptists stationed a disused railway coach that served as a tiny mission church. That must be getting on for a century ago; the coach's installation, as the late Mr Howard Williams used to say, was marked by the singing of a specially composed hymn – 'It was a happy day when the Lord to Doniford came'. A meter that sounds a trifle awkward to wed to a tune!

The Doniford picture began to change with the cessation of the lime-burning industry, and the donkeys were not retained for children's beach rides! But it remained Williton's seaside, and the horses and carts used the slipway to bring up shingle. The little boats came no more to the mooring posts, and one morning in the 1920s, following a tempestuous night, the cry rang through Williton, 'Doniford slip's been washed away'. Thus began, violently, a process of erosion that has gone on to the present day, though more slowly in recent years. When the slipway, the donkey houses, and a large face of cliff fell prey to Neptune, the wide cart track access to the cliffs and beach past the lime-kilns was closed, and remained so for many years, but Williton's way to the sea was preserved by the creation of a fenced footpath alongside, leading to steps in a fissure of the cliff.

The sea having altered Doniford permanently by taking the slipway, the popularity of the beach ebbed for an entirely different reason. In the mid-1920s the Army came upon the scene. The cliff top strip to the west became an anti-aircraft practice gun park, where training and its results would one day play a vital part in the defence of our island shores. The peace of the beach was shattered for many years to come by the ear-splitting speech of the latest Ack-Ack guns (4.7s were they?). The dog roses in the old Doniford road hedges were entangled with the coloured communication wires that led to searchlight batteries on the hillsides around Williton – and the guns barked by day and night. From the cliff top, visited often by the 'top brass' in the last few smouldering years before 1939, was catapulted the 'Queen Bee', the pilotless radio-controlled aircraft that was a wonder of its day.

The cliff top reverberated, and the people of a shaken Watchet groaned and endured for more than 25 years. And then, one day, silence reigned, and has since gone unbroken. Nuclear warfare, science marching on with air missiles, had made the Ack-Ack guns of 1939–45 as obsolete as bows and arrows.

The grass grew on the gun park, the buildings left by the WD began to fret away, but it was a derliction that spelt a new tide of popularity for Doniford beach. The Parish Council negotiated for the re-opening of the old cart-track entrance by the lime-kilns, and established a small car park on the cliff (though it could do with proper surface), and regularly maintained the narrow pedestrian access through the cliff to the beach, down which the children of 1965 skedaddle so delightedly towards the rock-pools and the tide.

So, in a sense, the nuclear age and all its wonders and frightening possibilities restored Doniford beach to something of the attraction it held for our ancestors in a more leisured and less complicated age. The old home industries of limpet-picking and laver-making seemed to die out many years ago, and the only fishing is for fun, but on suitable afternoons the new Willitonians and the descendants of the old families pass down through the cliff defile to the uncomplicated pleasures of the homely beach.

Doniford or Dawlish tide – it makes no difference to the child. There is a word in Revelation – 'And there shall be no more sea'. Grown-ups cannot comprehend it; no child would appreciate it!

The military vacated Doniford Camp in 1970 and it was developed into a holiday complex. The West Somerset Railway have now established an official halt at Doniford.

Footnote: On Jumby Bay Island, Antigua, in the more exotic location of the Caribbean, is a residence called Doniford House. It is so named by former Williton boy Peter Swann after the many happy hours spent among the rock-pools on Doniford beach in his boyhood.

Doniford House, Jumby Bay Island, Antigua, residence of Peter Swann, who spent his boyhood at Williton.

Above: *Watery Lane, Doniford, c.1925. Note the watercress bed on right.*

Left: *Swillbridge, Doniford, showing the ancient water cross in the foreground, so called from its position near an old stream (the cottage on the right is now demolished), c.1920.*

Left: *Doniford Camp in the 1950s.*

Below: *The River Swill at Doniford, c.1930. The cottage on the right has now been demolished.*

Doniford Farmhouse (formerly a priest house), c.1930s.

Left: *The Jones girls of Rose Cottage, Doniford, c.1945. Left to right: Margaret, Eleanor ('Ginger'), Louise, Doreen.*

Doniford in the 1950s showing Rose Cottage on the right (later demolished by flood) and Bridge Cottage on the left (later demolished for improved traffic visibility).

Early days at Doniford gun park, c.1927.

Doniford's association with the military lasted for 45 years. In 1925 the War Department was looking for a suitable site for an anti-aircraft artillery range and they settled for the cliff top at Doniford, which became known as the gun park. The range was only used during the summer months until just before the outbreak of the Second World War when a permanent camp was established. In the early days a tented camp was set up at Liddymore (now the Liddymore estate). Among top brass who visited Doniford just before the outbreak of the Second World War were War Minister Leslie Hore-Belisha, leading defence generals, about 50 MPs, and mayors of 16 London boroughs who sought assurance that the Metropolis would not lack defence when the time came. As well as planes trailing targets there was the Queen Bee, the first radio-controlled plane,

which was also used for target practice by the gunners. The first Queen Bees were launched from the cruiser HMS *Neptune* anchored off Watchet, but were later catapulted from the gun park at Doniford and could be jinked about the sky to avoid shells – not always successfully. When hit it would crash into the sea to await recovery by the SS *Radstock* berthed in Watchet harbour *(pictured on page 28)*. Following the end of the war, Doniford camp was occupied by the RAF Regiment for anti-aircraft gunnery training. The ear-splitting noise of the gunfire ceased in the 1960s, the camp then being occupied by various Army regiments until closure in 1970. Generally speaking, local people and servicemen got along fairly well; quite a number of military men married local girls and after their service settled in the area.

Queen Bee N1841 mounted on the catapult at Doniford in 1938. It was built by de Havilland at Hatfield. The aircraft was propelled along a rotatable catapult operated by a mixture of compressed air and glycerine fired by a cordite charge. In total 387 Queen Bees were built as radio-controlled pilotless target drones.

Rydon and Wibble

Rydon Farm, early 1900s.

The 'Hurdy Gurdy' man, with his wife walking alongside, passing through Rydon in the 1930s. They would go from door to door selling pots and pans and offering to sharpen scissors or knives.

Wibble Farm, c.1950, now a garden nursery.

Rydon Lodge in the 1930s. The Lodge was built in 1861–62, reputedly incorporating some of the timbers of the old St Etheldreda's Church at St Audries and to commemorate the death of Prince Albert.

Stream

Stream mear, c.1905.

Above: *'The Poplars', Higher Stream, a former private school for girls.*

Right: *Reprinted from the* West Somerset Free Press, *1904.*

WILLITON SCHOOL for GIRLS,
THE POPLARS, STREAM, WILLITON.

CONDUCTED by the Misses GREEN. A limited number of Boarders received.

The Course of Study includes Religious Instruction, English, Languages, Mathematics, Natural Science, Needlework, Drawing, Painting, Music, and Singing.

Pupils prepared for Musical and other Public Examinations.

Pupils living at a distance can dine at the school at a moderate charge.

Boys under ten years of age admitted.

Full particulars on application to Miss GREEN, Stream.

Next Term will commence on MONDAY, SEPTEMBER 19th.

Bardon

Bardon Manor.

Part of the small yard at Bardon Manor, where cock fighting was said to have taken place.

On the outskirts of the old parish, Bardon Manor dates from the mid-sixteenth century and was occupied by the Leigh family later that century. The family remained tenants until purchasing the property from the Wyndham estate in 1919, but sold it in 1924. The Leighs practised as attorneys, which profession continued at the house for many years.

In 1834 papers relating to the imprisonment and trial of Mary Queen of Scots were discovered in the house. Legend has it that a white dove would repeatedly fly against a small attic window, breaking the glass. As a result of this, the attic was searched and among its contents was a small chest containing docu-

Right: *Line-drawing showing the Bardon legend, by Michael Chapman.*

Below: *The Leigh family coat of arms in a window at Bardon Manor.*

ments relating to the trial of Mary Queen of Scots, who was executed in 1587. In 1870 the British Museum acquired these valuable documents from Bardon. Well-known local playwright Phoebe Rees wrote a play on the subject entitled *The White Dove of Bardon*, which was broadcast on BBC radio. Among other Bardon legends and ghost stories is the sound of the Bardon coach and horses on the gravel drive on a winter's night, but never any sightings. The house was thatched until 1834, and the hall dates from 1550 and has an Anglo-Saxon herring-bone back fireplace. The Mediterranean pomegranate tree *(top left picture, right)* and Magnolia tree *(left)* are reputed to be over 100 years old.

The trunk of a 400-year-old chestnut tree in the grounds of Bardon Manor.

Subscribers

Les and Gill Allen, Williton, Somerset
Rev. Richard Allen, Williton
Chris E. Allison, Watchet, Somerset
Richard Amery
John and Jean Andow, Sundays River, Colchester, South Africa
Violet Ann (née James)
Betty and Peter Armstrong, Trull, Taunton
Clara Violet Babb, Watchet, Somerset
Miss Joyce Bacon, Watchet, Somerset
Amelia and Thomas Bale, Watchet
Malcolm and Glenda Bale, Watchet
June Barnes (Deceased), formerly of Higher Stream Farm, Williton
Malcolm and Denise Bemister, Chafford Hundred, Essex
Mr and Mrs M. Binding, Stretton, Burton Upon Trent
Dudley and Ann Binding, Watchet
In memory of Joyce and Jim Binding, Lowestoft, Suffolk
Mrs Dorothy I. Binding, Watchet, Somerset
Mr and Mrs Edward G. Bircham, Colorado Springs, USA
Keith and Ann Bishop, Williton
Richard Lee Boggie, Watchet, Somerset
Yvonne and John Bonser, Blue Anchor
Chris Boyles, Alcombe, Minehead, Somerset
Ray Braunton, Wellington, Shropshire
Aaron J. Brooksbank, Somerset
Malcolm and Grace Brown, Watchet, Somerset
John and Audrey Bruford, Taunton
David and Dilys Bryant, Greenway, Watchet, Somerset
David Bulpin, Williton, Somerset
E. Geoffrey Burgess
Jane Butland and Stephen Sharp, Watchet, Somerset
William Challice, BEM, Watchet Ambulance
Mike and Wendy Chapman, Yeovil, Somerset
Roy and Helen Chave, Watchet, Somerset

Vera Chidgey, Williton, Somerset
The Lady Chidgey, Alresford, Hampshire
The Lord Chidgey, of Hamble-le-Rice, Alresford, Hampshire
Desmond Kenneth Chidgey, Cardiff
The Honourable Joanna L. Chidgey, London
The Honourable Caitlin V. Chidgey, London
The Honourable David R. Chidgey, London
Mrs Phyllis M. Chidgey, Williton, Somerset
Maurice and Joyce Chidgey (née Chave), Watchet, Somerset
Gay Chilcott, Watchet, Somerset
Sheila and Angela Chubb, Watchet, Somerset
Felicity Clarke, Watchet, Somerset
Mr Tony Clausen, Watchet, Somerset
Sheila and Eric Clavey, Watchet, Somerset
Paul Clavey, Watchet, Somerset
Chris Cooke, Watchet, Somerset
Sandra and John Coombs, Williton, Somerset
Kirsty Cornish (née Knight), Watchet
Sharon Costley (née Meader), Watchet
Helen A. and Claire R. Cridge, Watchet, Somerset
Thelma E. Cull, Wimborne, Dorset
Michael and Valerie Dan, Watchet
Alec Danby, Town Crier, Watchet
Valerie Davies (née Hopkins), Bristol
Annette Dickinson (née Chidgey), Samuel Dickinson & Lee Graham, Exeter, Devon
Grace Dixon (née Lyddon)
Pauline and Gary Dyer, Five Bells, Watchet, Somerset
Mollie G. Edbrooke (née Penny)
P.D. Edwards, Old Cleeve
David Edwards, Williton
James Edwards, Bishops Lydeard
Simon and Alison Farmer, Portishead, Bristol
Mrs C.A. Fiddes, Bourne, Lincs
Kally Finch, Watchet, Somerset

Geraldine Fuller (née Williams), Bishops Lydeard, Somerset

The Gardner Family, Almyer Terr, Watchet

Sue and Tony Gay, Swillbridge House, Doniford

Margaret V. Gould, Dunster

Phillipa Graham (née Woolley), Bournemouth

David and Pat Groves, Portishead

Iris M. Haller (née Coombs), Taunton

Roger, Frances and Sally Ham, Watchet

Liz Hamshere, Watchet, Somerset

Brenda Jean Harris, Williton, Somerset

Jenny Hill, Watchet, Somerset

Kenneth E. Holness

Dawn Hornby, Watchet

House, Sutton, Rayner, formerly Almyr Terrace, Watchet

Mr Bryan Howe, Minehead

Mr David Howe, Thatcham

Mrs Jean Howe MBE

Derek and Cheryl Howells, Williton

Craig, Linda and Bradley Howells, Watchet

Inez Hubbard (née Jones), Peterborough

Wendy Hubbard (née Luck), Conington, Peterborough

Dr Julian B. Hunt, Virginia Water, Surrey

Violet M. James, Watchet, Somerset

Joan G. Jones

Mrs Gina Kemp, Watchet, Somerset

Tony Knight, Watchet

Judy Kyte (née McMillan), Watchet and Taunton

Wendy Land (née Williams), Bridgwater, Somerset

David J. Langdon, Williton, Somerset

Dave and Pam Laws, Watchet, Somerset

Mrs Peggy Leach

Michael Leat, Bristol

Mr J. Lee, Shepton Mallet, Somerset

Mr Julian C. Locke, Tottenham, London

Mr Adrian J. Locke, Tottenham, London

Mrs Elizabeth Lyddon, Taunton, Somerset

Donald H. Mattravers, Weston Zoyland, Somerset

Doreen Mayo (née Davis), Watchet

Diana McDermaid (née Jones), Peterborough

Stuart McMillan, Watchet and Penarth

Clara E. Mead (née Wilkins), Born Watchet 1876, died Bristol 1966

Alan Middleton Gale, Williton, Somerset

Mr David and Mrs Daphne Milton

John Morse, Berkhamsted, Herts

Liz and Pete Murphy, Watchet

Frances Napper, Kilve, Somerset

Dibby Nethercott, St Audries

Barry New, Portsmouth, Hants

James L. Nicholas, Watchet, Somerset

Colin Norman, Watchet

Keith Ivor Norman, Watchet, Somerset

Barry Norman, Bristol

Ben and Margaret Norman, Watchet, Somerset

Katie Norman (née Knight), Watchet

Mrs Audrey Palmer (née Chilcott), Williton, Somerset

Mary Parkman (House), formerly Alymyr Terrace, Watchet

Stuart, Marie, William, Declan and Connor Paterson, Watchet, Somerset

Pamela Perkins, Watchet, Somerset

Stephen and Lisa Plenty (née Chidgey), Ethan and Ebony Plenty, Alcombe, Minehead, Somerset

E. Basil Poole, Aldridge, Walsall

Ashleigh-Jane Potter, Williton

Jennie Priscott (née Stronach), Watchet

Brian Redd, Washford

Les Reeder, Watchet, Somerset

Ray Richards, Williton

Mr F. Richards, now of Doniford

Sheila and Ray Rigglesford, London

Eileen and Roger Risdon, Williton, Somerset

Ken and June Roberts (née Stone), Watchet, Somerset

Adrian G. Rowe, Watchet, Somerset

Elva Seldon (née Willicombe)

Roy Shopland, Ottery St Mary, Devon

B. And J.M. Skudder, Doniford

Mrs M. Slade, Williton

Vivian Spence, Doniford

John and Joyce Spoor, Watchet, Somerset

Duncan Stafford, St Audries

Mr Martin G. Stevens, Watchet, Somerset

Lilian F. Stevens Downer, Watchet, Somerset

Stock family, Formerly of Watchet

Gladys Stone, South Yardley, Birmingham

Mr William F.H. Stone, East Quantoxhead, Somerset

David and Shirley Sully, Williton, Somerset
Martin R. Sutton, Arundel, West Sussex
Ronald E. Takel, Cwmbran, Gwent
Mark Taylor, Caterham, Surrey (formerly Williton, Somerset)
Colin, William and Rebecca Tennant
John and Heather Tennant
Diana Tipper (née McMillan), Watchet and Taunton
Nathan, Ginnette, Alex, Ben and Fern Towells, Watchet
Joy and Keith Towells, Watchet
Sue Upstone, Watchet, Somerset
W.C. and A. M. Vaughan, Williton
John F.W. Walling, Newton Abbot, Devon
Mr Stephen and Mrs Christine Waterman, Liddymore Road, Watchet
Geoffrey and Margaret Watts, Watchet

Evelyn L. Watts, Isle of Wight
Peggy Wheel (née Morse)
Peter M. White, Honiton, Devon
Joy L. Whittington, Watchet
Ray and Sue Whittington, and Roxanne Langdon, Williton
Clayton and Sally Williams, Watchet
Geoffrey M. Williams, Linton, Old Cleeve
Alan and Peggy Williams, Uxbridge, Canada
Mrs Shirley Williams, Williton, Somerset
Sue Williams (née Hurley), Bridgwater, Somerset
Gordon Willicombe, Cheltenham
Gill and Moger Woolley, Winterbourne
Andrew Woolley, Cookham-Dean
Mrs Audrey Young, Slough, Berkshire

Further Titles

For information regarding up-to-date availability,
please check our website at www.halsgrove.com

The Book of Addiscombe • Canning and Clyde Road
Residents Association and Friends
The Book of Addiscombe, Vol. II • Canning and Clyde Road
Residents Association and Friends
The Book of Ashburton • Stuart Hands and Pete Webb
The Book of Axminster with Kilmington • Les Berry
and Gerald Gosling
The Book of Axmouth & the Undercliff •
Ted Gosling and Mike Clement
The Book of Bakewell • Trevor Brighton
The Book of Bampton • Caroline Seward
The Book of Barnstaple • Avril Stone
The Book of Barnstaple, Vol. II • Avril Stone
The Book of Beaminster • Beaminster Museum
The Book of The Bedwyns • Bedwyn History Society
The Book of Bere Regis • Rodney Legg and John Pitfield
The Book of Bergh Apton • Geoffrey I. Kelly
The Book of Bickington • Stuart Hands
The Book of Bideford • Peter Christie and Alison Grant
Blandford Forum: A Millennium Portrait • Blandford Forum
Town Council
The Book of Bitterne • Bitterne Local Historical Society
The Book of Blofield • Barbara Pilch
The Book of Boscastle • Rod and Anne Knight
The Book of Bourton-on-the-Hill, Batsford and Sezincote •
Allen Firth
The Book of Bramford • Bramford Local History Group
The Book of Breage & Germoe • Stephen Polglase
The Book of Bridestowe • D. Richard Cann
The Book of Bridgwater • Roger Evans
The Book of Bridport • Rodney Legg
The Book of Brixham • Frank Pearce
The Book of Brundall • Barbara Ayers and Group
The Book of Buckfastleigh • Sandra Coleman
The Book of Buckland Monachorum & Yelverton •
Pauline Hamilton-Leggett
The Book of Budleigh Salterton • D. Richard Cann
The Book of Carharrack • Carharrack Old
Cornwall Society
The Book of Carshalton • Stella Wilks and Gordon
Rookledge

The Book of Carhampton • Hilary Binding
The Parish Book of Cerne Abbas • Vivian and
Patricia Vale
The Book of Chagford • Iain Rice
The Book of Chapel-en-le-Frith • Mike Smith
*The Book of Chittlehamholt with
Warkleigh & Satterleigh* • Richard Lethbridge
The Book of Chittlehampton • Various
The Book of Codford • Romy Wyeth
The Book of Colney Heath • Bryan Lilley
The Book of Constantine • Moore and Trethowan
The Book of Cornwood and Lutton • Compiled by
the People of the Parish
The Book of Crediton • John Heal
The Book of Creech St Michael • June Small
The Book of Crowcombe, Bicknoller and Sampford Brett •
Maurice and Joyce Chidgey
The Book of Crudwell • Tony Pain
The Book of Cullompton • Compiled by the People
of the Parish
The Second Book of Cullompton • Compiled by the People
of the Parish
The Book of Dawlish • Frank Pearce
*The Book of Dulverton, Brushford,
Bury & Exebridge* • Dulverton and District Civic Society
The Book of Dunster • Hilary Binding
The Book of Easton • Easton Village History Project
The Book of Edale • Gordon Miller
The Ellacombe Book • Sydney R. Langmead
The Book of Elmsett • Elmsett Local History Group
The Book of Exmouth • W.H. Pascoe
The Book of Fareham • Lesley Burton and
Brian Musselwhite
The Book of Grampound with Creed • Bane and Oliver
The Book of Gosport • Lesley Burton and
Brian Musselwhite
The Book of Haughley • Howard Stephens
The Book of Hayle • Harry Pascoe
The Book of Hayling Island & Langstone • Peter Rogers
The Book of Helston • Jenkin with Carter
The Book of Hemyock • Clist and Dracott

❖ FURTHER TITLES ❖

The Book of Herne Hill • Patricia Jenkyns

The Book of Hethersett • Hethersett Society
Research Group

The Book of High Bickington • Avril Stone

The Book of Homersfield • Ken Palmer

The Book of Honiton • Gerald Gosling

The Book of Ilsington • Dick Wills

The Book of Kessingland • Maureen and Eric Long

The Book of Kingskerswell • Carsewella Local
History Group

The Book of Lamerton • Ann Cole and Friends

Lanner, A Cornish Mining Parish • Sharron
Schwartz and Roger Parker

The Book of Leigh & Bransford • Malcolm Scott

The Second Book of Leigh & Bransford • Malcolm Scott

The Book of Litcham with Lexham & Mileham • Litcham
Historical and Amenity Society

The Book of Llangain • Haydn Williams

The Book of Loddiswell • Loddiswell Parish History Group

The Book of Looe • Mark Camp

The New Book of Lostwithiel • Barbara Fraser

The Book of Lulworth • Rodney Legg

The Book of Lustleigh • Joe Crowdy

The Book of Lydford • Compiled by Barbara Weeks

The Book of Lyme Regis • Rodney Legg

The Book of Manaton • Compiled by the People
of the Parish

The Book of Markyate • Markyate Local History Society

The Book of Mawnan • Mawnan Local History Group

The Book of Meavy • Pauline Hemery

The Book of Mere • Dr David Longbourne

The Book of Minehead with Alcombe • Binding and Stevens

The Book of Monks Orchard and Eden Park • Ian Muir
and Pat Manning

The Book of Morchard Bishop • Jeff Kingaby

Mount Batten – The Flying Boats of Plymouth •
Gerald Wasley

The Book of Mulbarton • Jill and David Wright

The Book of Mylor • Mylor Local History Group

The Book of Narborough • Narborough Local
History Society

The Book of Newdigate • John Callcut

The Book of Newtown • Keir Foss

The Book of Nidderdale • Nidderdale Museum Society

The Book of Northlew with Ashbury • Northlew
History Group

The Book of North Newton • J.C. and K.C. Robins

The Book of North Tawton • Baker, Hoare and Shields

The Book of Notting Hill • Melvin Wilkinson

The Book of Nynehead • Nynehead & District
History Society

The Book of Okehampton • Roy and Ursula Radford

The Book of Ottery St Mary • Gerald Gosling and
Peter Harris

The Book of Paignton • Frank Pearce

The Book of Penge, Anerley & Crystal Palace •
Peter Abbott

The Book of Peter Tavy with Cudlipptown • Peter Tavy
Heritage Group

The Book of Pimperne • Jean Coull

The Book of Plymtree • Tony Eames

The Book of Poole • Rodney Legg

The Book of Porchfield & Locks Green • Keir Foss

The Book of Porlock • Dennis Corner

The Book of Portland • Rodney Legg

Postbridge – The Heart of Dartmoor • Reg Bellamy

The Book of Priddy • Albert Thompson

The Book of Princetown • Dr Gardner-Thorpe

The Book of Probus • Alan Kent and
Danny Merrifield

The Book of Rattery • By the People of the Parish

The Book of Roadwater, Leighland and Treborough •
Clare and Glyn Court

The Book of St Audries • Duncan Stafford

The Book of St Austell • Peter Hancock

The Book of St Day • Joseph Mills and Paul Annear

The Book of St Dennis and Goss Moor • Kenneth Rickard

The Book of St Ervan • Moira Tangye

The Book of St Levan • St Levan Local History Group

The Book of St Mawes • Chris Pollard

*The Book of Sampford Courtenay
with Honeychurch* • Stephanie Pouya

The Book of Sculthorpe • Gary Windeler

The Book of Seaton • Ted Gosling

The Book of Sennen • Alison Weeks and
Valerie Humphrys

The Book of Sidmouth • Ted Gosling and Sheila Luxton

The Book of Silverton • Silverton Local History Society

The Book of South Molton • Jonathan Edmunds

The Book of South Stoke with Midford • Edited by
Robert Parfitt

South Tawton & South Zeal with Sticklepath • Roy and
Ursula Radford

The Book of Sparkwell with Hemerdon & Lee Mill • Pam James